Workshop on Robust Unsupervised and Semisupervised Methods in Natural Language Processing 2011

(ROBUS 2011)

Held with the 8th International Conference on Recent Advances in Natural Language Processing 2011 (RANLP 2011)

Hissar, Bulgaria
15 September 2011

AA005731

ISBN: 978-1-62276-459-4

Printed from e-media with permission by:

Curran Associates, Inc.
57 Morehouse Lane
Red Hook, NY 12571

CURRAN ASSOCIATES INC. proceedings.com

Some format issues inherent in the e-media version may also appear in this print version.

Copyright© (2011) by the Association for Computational Linguistics
All rights reserved.

Printed by Curran Associates, Inc. (2012)

For permission requests, please contact the Association for Computational Linguistics at the address below.

Association for Computational Linguistics
209 N. Eighth Street
Stroudsburg, Pennsylvania 18360

Phone: 1-570-476-8006
Fax: 1-570-476-0860

acl@aclweb.org

Additional copies of this publication are available from:

Curran Associates, Inc.
57 Morehouse Lane
Red Hook, NY 12571 USA
Phone: 845-758-0400
Fax: 845-758-2634
Email: curran@proceedings.com
Web: www.proceedings.com

TABLE OF CONTENTS

Gibbs Sampling with Treeness Constraint in Unsupervised Dependency Parsing 1
David Marecek, Zdenek Zabokrtsky
Guided Self Training for Sentiment Classification 9
Brett Drury, Luis Torgo, J.J. Almedia
Investigating the Applicability of current Machine-Learning based Subjectivity Detection Algorithms on German Texts 17
Malik Atalla, Christian Scheel, Ernesto William De Luca, Sahin Albayrak
Learning to Extract Protein-Protein Interactions using Distant Supervision 25
Philippe Thomas, Illes Solt, Roman Klinger, Ulf Leser
Topic Models with Logical Constraints on Words 33
Hayato Kobayashi, Hiromi Wakaki, Tomohiro Yamasaki, Masaru Suzuki
Investigation of Co-training Views and Variations for Semantic Role Labeling 41
Rasoul Samad Zadeh Kaljahi, Mohd Sapiyan Baba
Author Index

Introduction

In natural language processing (NLP), supervised learning scenarios are more frequently explored than unsupervised or semi-supervised ones. Unfortunately, labeled data are often highly domain-dependent and short in supply. It has therefore become increasingly important to leverage both labeled and unlabeled data to achieve the best performance in challenging NLP problems that involve learning of structured variables.

Until recently most results in semi-supervised learning of structured variables in NLP were negative, but today the best part-of-speech taggers, named entity recognizers, and dependency parsers exploit mixtures of labeled and unlabeled data. Unsupervised and minimally unsupervised NLP also sees rapid growth.

The most commonly used semi-supervised learning algorithms in NLP are feature-based methods and EM, self- or co-training. Mixture models have also been successfully used. While feature-based methods seem relatively robust, self-training and co-training are very parameter-sensitive, and parameter tuning has therefore become an important research topic. This is not only a concern in NLP, but also in other areas such as face recognition. Parameter-sensitivity is even more dramatic in unsupervised learning of structured variables, e.g. unsupervised part-of-speech tagging and grammar induction.

The aim of this workshop was to bring together researchers dedicated to designing and evaluating robust unsupervised or semi-supervised learning algorithms for NLP problems. We received 11 papers, but accepted only six. Shane Bergsma gave an invited talk on feature-based methods.

The organizers would like to thank the review committee for their thorough high-quality reviews and their timeliness, and the RANLP 2011 organizers for their assistance.

Organizers:

Chris Biemann, TU Darmstadt
Anders Søgaard, University of Copenhagen

Program Committee:

Steven Abney, University of Michigan
Stefan Bordag, ExB Research & Development
Eugenie Giesbrecht, FZI Karlsruhe
Katja Filippova, Google
Florian Holz, University of Leipzig
Jonas Kuhn, University of Stuttgart
Vivi Nastase, HITS Heidelberg
Reinhard Rapp, JG University of Mainz
Lucia Specia, University of Wolverhampton
Valentin Spitkovsky, Stanford University
Sven Teresniak, University of Leipzig
Dekai Wu, HKUST
Torsten Zesch, TU Darmstadt
Jerry Zhu, University of Wisconsin-Madison

Invited Speaker:

Shane Bergsma, Johns Hopkins University

Gibbs Sampling with Treeness Constraint in Unsupervised Dependency Parsing

David Mareček and Zdeněk Žabokrtský
Charles University in Prague, Faculty of Mathematics and Physics
Institute of Formal and Applied Linguistics
{marecek,zabokrtsky}@ufal.mff.cuni.cz

Abstract

This paper presents a work in progress on the task of unsupervised parsing, following the main stream approach of optimizing the overall probability of the corpus. We evaluate a sequence of experiments for Czech with various modifications of corpus initiation, of dependency edge probability model and of sampling procedure, stressing especially the treeness constraint. The best configuration is then applied to 19 languages from CoNLL-2006 and CoNLL-2007 shared tasks. Our best achieved results are comparable to the state of the art in dependency parsing and outperform the previously published results for many languages.

1 Introduction

Unsupervised approaches receive considerably growing attention in NLP in the last years, and dependency parsing is not an exception.

In recent years, quite a lot of works in unsupervised parsing (or grammar induction) was based on Dependency Model with Valence (DMV) introduced by (Klein and Manning, 2004); (Smith, 2007) and (Cohen et al., 2008) has focused on DMV variants, (Headden et al., 2009) introduced extended valency model (EVG) and added lexicalization and smoothing. (Spitkovsky et al., 2011b) used punctuation marks for splitting a sentence and impose parsing restrictions over its fragments. Gibbs sampling was used in (Naseem and Barzilay, 2011).

Some of the papers focused on English only, but some presented the results across wide rage of languages. The last such paper was (Spitkovsky et al., 2011a), where the evaluation was done on all 19 languages included in CoNLL shared tasks (Buchholz and Marsi, 2006) and (Nivre et al., 2007). The attachment scores are very high for English, for which the methods seems to be optimized, but the scores are quite low for some other languages.

In this paper, we describe our new approach to unsupervised dependency parsing. Unlike DMV, it is not based on constituency trees, which cannot handle non-projectivities. We have been inspired rather by the experiment described in (Brody, 2010), in which the dependency parsing task is formulated as a problem of word alignment; every sentence is aligned with itself with one constraint: no word can be attached to itself. However, unlike (Brody, 2010), where the output structures might not be trees and could contain cycles, we introduce a sampling method with the acyclicity constraint.

Our approach attempts at optimizing the overall probability of tree structures given the corpus. We perform the optimization using Gibbs sampling (Gilks et al., 1996).

We employ several ways of incorporating prior knowledge about dependency trees into the system:

- independence assumptions – we approximate probability of a tree by a product of probabilities of dependency edges,
- edge models and feature selection – we use words' distance and their POS tags as the main indicators for predicting a dependency relation,
- hard constraints – some knowledge on dependency tree properties (such as acyclicity) is difficult to represent by local models, therefore we implement it as a hard constraint in the sampling procedure,
- corpus initialization – we study the effect of different initializations of trees in the corpus,

- basic linguistic assumptions – according to the dependency syntax tradition, we expect the trees to be verbocentric. This is done without determining which part-of-speech tag is what.

All experiments are evaluated in detail using Czech data. The configuration which performs best for Czech is applied also on other languages available in the CoNLL shared task corpora (Buchholz and Marsi, 2006) and (Nivre et al., 2007). Our goal is to achieve good results across various languages without tuning the parser individually for each language, so we use the other language data exclusively for evaluation purposes.

2 Data preparation

We used Czech training part (`dtrain.conll`) from CoNLL 2007 collection, which corresponds to approximately one third of Prague Dependency Treebank 2.0 (Hajič and others, 2006), PDT in the sequel. We selected all sentences containing at most 15 words after removing punctuation.[1] The resulting data contains 123,804 words in 14,766 sentences (out of 368,640 words and 25,360 sentences in the original `dtrain.conll` file).

We are aware of a strong bias caused by this filtering. For instance, it leads to a considerably higher proportion of sentences without a verb (such as titles – recall that PDT contains mainly newspaper articles). However, such filtering is a usual practise in unsupervised parsing due to time complexity issues.

Since Czech is a morphologically rich language, there are around 3,000 morphological tags distinguished in PDT. They consist of 15 positions, each of them corresponding to one morphological category. In the CoNLL format, Czech positional tags are distributed into three columns: CPOS (first position), POS (second position), and FEATURES (third to fifteenth position). For the purpose of unsupervised parsing experiments, we reduce the tag set at two levels of granularity:

- *CoarsePOS* – only the first letter is considered for each tag (11 distinct values, such as `V` for verbs and `P` for pronouns),

- *FinePOS* – only the first (coarse-grained POS) and the fifth letter (morphological case) is used if case is defined (such as `N4` for nouns in accusative), or the first and the second letter otherwise (such as `Vf` for infinitive verb forms); there are 58 distinct values.[2]

We use this data in all our tuning experiments (Sections 6.2 – 6.5). The final evaluation on CoNLL (Section 6.6) is different. It is made on all the sentences (without length limit) and only CoNLL POS tags are used there.

3 Models

Similarly to (Brody, 2010), we use two models which are very close to IBM Model 1 and 2 for word alignment (Brown et al., 1993). We do not model fertility (IBM Model 3), but we plan to involve it in future work. We introduce another model (called *NounRoot*) that postulates verbocentricity of the dependency trees and tries to repress Noun-Root dependencies.

3.1 Standard Dependency Models

In our models, each possible dependency edge is characterized by three attributes:

- T^g – tag of the governing node,

- T^d – tag of the dependent node,

- $D^{d,g}$ – signed distance between governing and dependent word (it is negative, if the dependent word precedes the governing one, and is equal to 0 if the governing node is the technical root).

The first model (called *Dep*) postulates that the tag of the governing node depends only on the tag of the dependent node. The probability that the node d is attached below the node g is:

$$P(d \rightarrow g) = P(T^g|T^d) = \frac{P(T^g, T^d)}{P(T^d)} \quad (1)$$

We assume that the dependencies follow a Chinese Restaurant Process (Aldous, 1985), in which the probability $P(T^g|T^d)$ is proportional to the number of times T^g have governed T^d in the past, as follows:

$$P(T_i^g|T_i^d) = \frac{count^{(-i)}(T_i^g, T_i^d) + \alpha_1}{count^{(-i)}(T_i^d) + \alpha_1|T|}, \quad (2)$$

[1] If a removed punctuation node was not a leaf, its children were attached below the removed node's parent. This occurs mainly with coordinations without conjunctions.

[2] This shape of tags has been previously shown to perform well for supervised parsing.

where the index i corresponds to the position of the dependent word in the corpus, $count^{(-i)}$ represents number of occurrences in the history (from 1 to $i-1$), $|T|$ is the number of tags in the tag set and α_1 is the Dirichlet hyper-parameter.

The second model (called *Dist*) assumes that the length of the dependency edge depends on the tag of the dependent node:

$$P(d \to g) = P(D^{d,g}|T^d) = \frac{P(D^{d,g}, T^d)}{P(T^d)} \quad (3)$$

$$P(D_i|T_i^d) = \frac{count^{(-i)}(D_i, T_i^d) + \alpha_2}{count^{(-i)}(T_i^d) + \alpha_2|D|}, \quad (4)$$

where $|D|$ is the number of all possible distances in the corpus. This number was set to 30.

The probability of a particular analysis (i.e., the probability of all dependency trees $\mathcal{T}$ built on a whole given corpus $\mathcal{C}$) can be computed as:

$$\begin{aligned} P(\mathcal{C}, \mathcal{T}) &= \prod_{i=1}^{N} P(T_i^g|T_i^d) \cdot P(D_i|T_i^d) \\ &= \prod_{i=1}^{N} \left(\frac{count^{(-i)}(T_i^g, T_i^d) + \alpha_1}{count^{(-i)}(T_i^d) + \alpha_1|T|} \right. \quad (5) \\ &\qquad \left. \frac{count^{(-i)}(D_i, T_i^d) + \alpha_2}{count^{(-i)}(T_i^d) + \alpha_2|D|} \right) \end{aligned}$$

We maximize this probability using Gibbs sampling (Gilks et al., 1996).

3.2 Noun-Root Dependency Repression

During our first experiments, we noticed that nouns (especially subjects) often substitute verbs in the governing positions. Since majority of grammars are verbocentric (verbs dominates their subjects and objects), we decided to penalize noun-root edges. Of course, we do not want to state explicitly which tag represents nouns in a particular tag set. Instead, nouns are recognized automatically as the most frequent coarse-grained tag category in the corpus (this simple rule holds for all languages in the CoNLL 2006 and 2007 sets).[3] We add the following model called *Noun-Root*:

$$P(d \to g) = \begin{cases} \beta & \text{if } d \text{ is noun and } g \text{ is root} \\ 1 & \text{otherwise} \end{cases} \quad (6)$$

[3]We are aware that introducing this rule is a kind of hack, which departs from the line of purely unsupervised parsing and which will become useless with automatically induced POS tags in future experiments. On the other hand, this simple trick has a substantial effect on parsing quality. Therefore we decided to present results both with and without using it.

This model is added into the product in Equation (5). The value of β was experimentally set to 0.01.

4 Sampling

We sample from the posterior distribution of our model $P(T^g, D^{g,d}|T^d)$ using Gibbs sampling (a standard Markov chain Monte Carlo technique). We sample each dependency edge independently. Computing the conditional probabilities is straightforward, because the numerators and denominators in the product in Equation (5) are exchangeable. If we substitute the parent of a word by a new parent, we can deal with the dependency as if it were the last one in the corpus. The history remains unchanged and updating the probability is thus very efficient.

4.1 Basic sampling algorithm

The pseudocode of the basic sampling algorithm is shown in Figure 1. This algorithm chooses one parent for each word. It may create cycles and discontinuous directed graphs; such graphs are also accepted as the algorithm's initial input.

```
iterate {
  foreach sentence {
    foreach node in rand_permutation_of_nodes {

      # estimate probability of node's parents
      foreach parent in (0 .. |sentence|) {
        next if parent == node;
        node->set_parent(parent);
        prob[parent] = estimate_edge_prob();
      }

      # choose parent w.r.t. the distribution
      parent = sample from prob[parent];
      node->set_parent(parent);
    }
  }
}
```

Figure 1: Pseudo-code of the basic sampling approach (cycles are allowed).

4.2 Hard Constraints

The problem of the basic sampling algorithm is that it does not sample trees. It only chooses a parent for each word but does not guarantee the acyclicity. We introduce and explore two hard constraints:

- *Tree* – for each sentence, the set of assigned edges constitutes a tree in all phases of computation,[4]

[4]This constraint is not compliant with the *RandInit* initialization.

- *SingleRoot* – the technical root can have only one child.

Tree-sampling algorithm with pseudocode in Figure 2 ensures the treeness of the sampled structures. It is more complicated, because it checks acyclicity after each sampled edge. If there is a cycle, it chooses one edge which will be deleted and the remaining node is then hanged on another node so that no other cycle is created. This deletion and rehanging is done using the same sampling method.

```
iterate {
  foreach sentence {
    foreach node in rand_permutation_of_nodes {

      # estimate probability of node's parents
      foreach parent in (0 .. |sentence|) {
        next if parent == node;
        node->set_parent(parent);
        prob[parent] = estimate_edge_prob();
      }

      # choose parent w.r.t. the distribution
      parent = sample from prob[parent];
      node->set_parent(parent);

      if (cycle was created) {

        # choose where to break the cycle
        foreach node2 in cycle {
          parent = node2->parent;
          node2->unset_parent();
          prob[node2] = estimate_edge_prob();
          node2->set_parent(parent);
        }
        node2 = sample from prob[node2];

        # choose the new parent
        foreach parent {
          next if node2->parent creates a cycle
          node2->set_parent(parent);
          prob[parent] =  estimate_edge_prob();
        }
        parent = sample from prob[parent];
        node2->set_parent(parent);
      }
    }
  }
}
```

Figure 2: Pseudo-code of the tree-sampling approach (cycles are not allowed).

The second hard constraint represents the fertility of the technical root, which is generally supposed to be low. Ideally, each sentence should have one word which dominates all other words. For this reason, we allow only one word to depend on the technical root. If the root acquires two children during sampling, one of them is immediately resampled (a new parent is sampled for the child).

5 Experimental Setup

This section describes the ways of initialization, and how the final dependency trees are built from sampling.

5.1 Corpus Initialization

We implemented four different procedures for initiating dependency edges in the corpus:

- *RandInit* – each word is attached below a randomly chosen word from the same sentence (or the technical root); treeness is not ensured,
- *RandTreeInit* – like *RandInit*, but treeness is ensured (only edges not leading to a cycle are added),
- *LeftChainInit* – in each sentence, each word is attached below its left neighbor; the first word is attached below the technical root,
- *RightChainInit* – each word is attached below its right neighbor; the last word is attached below the technical root.

The last two are used only for computing the baseline scores.

5.2 Dirichlet hyper-parameters

Following (Brody, 2010), we set the Dirichlet hyper-parameters α_1 and α_2 to values 0.01 and 0.05 respectively. We did not optimize the values carefully because our preliminary experiments confirm the observation of (Brody, 2010): limited variations (up to an order of magnitude) in these parameters have only a negligible effect on the final results.

5.3 Number of iterations

Experiments showed that the sampling algorithm makes only little changes of probabilities after the 30th iteration (see the Figure 3). All the experiments were running with 30 "burn-in" iterations and then other 20 iterations from which the final dependency trees were computed.

5.4 Parsing

We can simply take the trees after the last iteration and declare them as a result. A better way is, however, take the last (in our case 20) iterations and create an average trees (or average directed graphs). We tested two procedures for creating an average tree (or graph) from n different trees (graphs):

- *Max* – We attach each node to its most frequent parent. This method allows cycles.

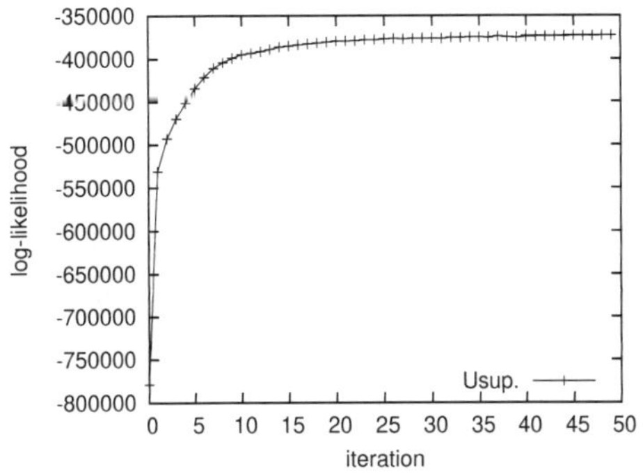

Figure 3: Log-likelihoods of the data through 50 iterations. An example of one run.

- *MST* – Each edge has a weight proportional to the number of times it appeared during the iterations. A maximum spanning tree algorithm (Chu and Liu, 1965) is then applied on each sentence. This method always creates trees.

6 Experiments and Evaluation

6.1 Evaluation metrics

As in other unsupervised tasks (e.g. in unsupervised POS induction), there is a little consensus on evaluation measures. Performance of unsupervised methods is often measured by comparing the induced outputs with gold standard manual annotations. However, this approach causes a general problem: manual annotation is inevitably guided by a number of conventions, such as the traditional POS categories in unsupervised POS tagging, or varying (often linguistically controversial) conventions for local tree shapes representing e.g. complex verb forms in unsupervised dependency parsing. It is obvious that using unlabeled attachment scores (UAS) leads to a strong bias towards such conventions and it might not be a good indicator of unsupervised parsing improvements. Therefore we estimate parsing quality by two additional metrics:

- UUAS - undirected UAS (edge direction is disregarded),

- NED - neutral edge direction, introduced in (Schwartz et al., 2011), which treats not only a node's gold parent and child as the correct answer, but also its gold grandparent.

6.2 Baseline and upper bound estimates

We evaluate four baselines straightforwardly corresponding to four corpus initiation procedures described in Section 5.1: *RandBaseline*, *RandTree-Baseline*, *LeftChainBaseline*, and *RightChain-Baseline*.

In order to have an upper bound limit, we use Ryan McDonald's implementation of Maximum Spanning Tree parser (McDonald et al., 2005) (*SupervisedMST*). Only features based on reduced POS tags are accessible to the parser. We use the data described in Section 2 both for training and evaluation in the 10-fold cross-validation fashion and present the average result.

The results of the baseline and upper bound experiments are summarized in Table 1.

Parser	Tags	UAS	UUAS	NED
RandBaseline	–	12.0	19.9	27.5
RandTreeB.	–	11.9	21.0	31.0
LeftChainB.	–	30.2	53.6	67.2
RightChainB.	–	25.5	52.0	60.6
SupervisedMST	CoarsePOS	73.9	78.6	86.6
SupervisedMST	FinePOS	82.5	84.9	90.3

Table 1: Lower and upper bounds for unsupervised parsing of Czech based on reduced POS tags.

6.3 Results for Czech

Selected experiments and results for Czech are summarized in Table 2. We started with a simple configuration without sampling constraints. Then we were gradually adding our improvements and constraints: *MST* parsing, *Tree* and *SingleRoot* constraint and *NounRoot* model. Everything was measured both for *CoarsePOS* and *FinePOS* tags and evaluated with all three measures.

We can see that CoarsePOS tags work better if we do not use *SingleRoot* constraint or *Noun-Root* model. Adding *NounRoot* model improves the *UAS* by 8 percent. We choose the settings of the experiment number 10 (which uses all our improvements and constraints) as the best configuration for Czech. It has the highest *UUAS* score and the values of the other scores are very close to the maximum achieved values.

6.4 Learning curves

It is useful to draw learning curves in order to see how well the learning algorithm can exploit additional data. Figure 4 shows the speed of growth of UAS for our best unsupervised configuration in

n.	Initialization	Tags	Models	Constraints	Parsing	UAS	UUAS	NED
Baseline configuration:								
1	Random	CoarsePOS	Dep+Dist	–	Max	45.1	51.2	55.8
2	Random	FinePOS	Dep+Dist	–	Max	41.3	47.6	51.0
Parsing with Maximum spanning tree algorithm:								
3	Random	CoarsePOS	Dep+Dist	–	MST	44.8	58.8	67.1
4	Random	FinePOS	Dep+Dist	–	MST	36.7	50.1	55.1
Using tree-sampling:								
5	RandomTree	CoarsePOS	Dep+Dist	Tree	MST	45.5	55.1	59.5
6	RandomTree	FinePOS	Dep+Dist	Tree	MST	36.2	46.6	50.0
Single-root constraint added:								
7	RandomTree	CoarsePOS	Dep+Dist	Tree+SingleRoot	MST	41.8	58.9	72.2
8	RandomTree	FinePOS	Dep+Dist	Tree+SingleRoot	MST	41.2	58.6	70.8
Noun-Root repression model added:								
9	RandomTree	CoarsePOS	Dep+Dist+NounRoot	Tree+SingleRoot	MST	49.6	62.2	**73.3**
10	RandomTree	FinePOS	Dep+Dist+NounRoot	Tree+SingleRoot	MST	49.8	**62.6**	73.0
Experiments with constraints on the best configuration:								
11	RandomTree	FinePOS	Dep+Dist+NounRoot	–	MST	42.0	56.3	62.8
12	RandomTree	CoarsePOS	Dep+Dist+NounRoot	Tree	MST	**50.0**	59.8	66.9
13	RandomTree	FinePOS	Dep+Dist+NounRoot	Tree	MST	46.8	55.9	61.1
14	RandomTree	FinePOS	Dep+Dist+NounRoot	SingleRoot	MST	40.8	58.0	66.6
Other selected experiments:								
15	RandomTree	FinePOS	Dep+Dist+NounRoot	–	Max	45.1	51.2	55.8
16	RandomTree	FinePOS	Dep+Dist+NounRoot	–	Max	44.6	50.5	53.0
17	RandomTree	FinePOS	Dep+Dist+NounRoot	Tree+SingleRoot	Max	49.9	62.5	72.8

Table 2: Evaluation of different configurations of the unsupervised parser for Czech.

comparison with the supervised parser (evaluated by 10-fold cross validation, again).

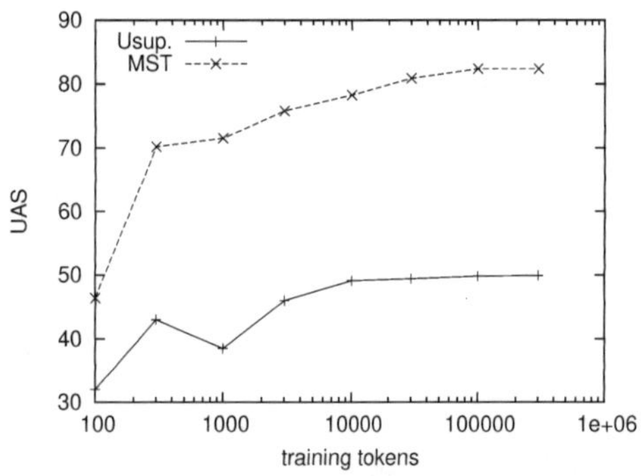

Figure 4: Learning curves for Czech: UAS of unsupervised (our best configuration) and supervised (unlexicalized McDonald's MST) parsers as functions of data size. *FinePOS* tags were used.

One can see that from 10,000 tokens the *UAS* for our best configuration grows very little and we do not need more data if we are dealing with POS tags only. We suppose that more data would be needed when using lexicalization.

6.5 Error analysis

Table 3 shows attachment scores for individual coarse-grained Czech POS tags. One can see very low UAS values with particles, interjections, and punctuation (special characters not filtered in the preprocessing step), however, these categories are not frequent in the corpus. Prepositions and conjunctions are more frequent, but their attachment score is still only 20.4% and 14.2% respectively. This fact is caused mainly by reversed dependencies; our parser attaches prepositions below nouns and conjunctions below verbs, while in the corpus, prepositions dominate nouns and conjunctions dominate verbs. These reversed dependencies are treated as correct with UUAS and NED measures.

CPOS	Occurrences	UAS [%]	Err. [%]
N (nouns)	21934	48.5	18.8
A (adjectives)	12890	80.1	2.6
V (verbs)	10946	55.1	7.2
P (pronouns)	6294	66.2	2.6
D (adverbs)	4025	49.4	3.3
R (prepositions)	2596	20.4	8.2
C (numerals)	1884	40.5	2.2
J (conjunctions)	957	14.2	4.7
T (particles)	198	23.6	0.5
I (interjections)	5	27.8	0.0
Z (punctuation)	3	18.8	0.0

Table 3: UAS for individual coarse-grained Czech POS tags. The "*Err.*" column shows the percentage of errors on the whole corpus.

Nouns make most errors in total, especially in the longer noun phrases, where the correct struc-

Language			Baselines			Results			
name	code	CoNLL	rand.	left	right	Our-NR	Our	Spi5	Spi6
Arabic	ar	2007	3.9	59.0	6.0	24.8	25.0	22.0	**49.5**
Bulgarian	bg	2006	8.0	38.8	17.9	**51.4**	25.4	44.3	43.9
Catalan	ca	2007	3.9	30.0	24.8	56.3	55.3	**63.8**	59.8
Czech	cs	2007	7.4	29.6	24.2	**33.3**	24.3	31.4	28.4
Danish	da	2006	6.7	47.8	13.1	38.6	30.2	**44.0**	38.3
German	de	2006	7.2	22.0	23.4	21.8	26.7	**33.5**	30.4
Greek	el	2007	4.9	19.7	31.4	33.4	**39.0**	21.4	13.2
English	en	2007	4.4	21.0	29.4	23.8	24.0	34.9	**45.2**
Spanish	es	2006	4.3	29.8	24.7	**54.6**	53.0	33.3	50.6
Basque	eu	2007	11.1	23.0	30.5	34.7	29.1	**43.6**	24.0
Hungarian	hu	2007	6.5	5.5	41.4	**48.1**	48.0	23.0	34.7
Italian	it	2007	4.2	37.4	21.6	**60.6**	57.5	37.6	52.3
Japanese	ja	2006	14.2	13.8	67.2	**53.5**	52.2	**53.5**	50.2
Dutch	nl	2006	7.5	24.5	28.0	**43.4**	32.2	32.5	27.8
Portugese	pt	2006	5.8	31.2	25.8	41.8	**43.2**	34.4	36.7
Slovenian	sl	2006	7.9	26.6	24.3	**34.6**	25.4	33.6	32.2
Swedish	sv	2006	7.8	27.8	25.9	26.9	23.3	42.5	**50.0**
Turkish	tr	2006	6.4	1.5	65.4	32.1	32.2	33.4	**35.9**
Chinese	zh	2007	15.3	13.4	41.3	34.6	21.0	34.5	**43.2**
		Average:	7.2	26.4	29.8	**39.4**	35.1	36.7	39.3

Table 4: Directed unlabeled attachment scores for 19 different languages from CoNLL shared task. The "rand.", "left", and "right" columns reports *Random*, *LeftChain*, and *RightChain* baselines. The "Our-NR" and "Our" columns show results of our algorithm; "NR" means that Noun-Root dependency suppression was used. For comparison, "Spi5" and "Spi6" are the results reported in (Spitkovsky et al., 2011a) in Tables 5 and 6 respectively.

ture cannot be induced from POS tags only. On the other hand, adjectives reach as much as 80% UAS.

6.6 Results for CoNLL languages

We applied our unsupervised dependency parser on all languages included in 2006 and 2007 CoNLL shared tasks. We used the configuration that was the best for Czech (experiment 10 in Table 2) and the same configuration without using Noun-Root dependency repression (experiment 8). The parsing was run on concatenated trainining and development sets[5] after removing punctuation, but the final attachment scores were measured on the development sets only, so that they were comparable to the previously reported results. Unlike in 6.3, there is no sentence length limit and the evaluation is done for all the sentences and only the *POS* (fifth column in the CoNLL format) is used for the inference.

The results are shown in Table 4. The *Random*, *LeftChain*, and *RightChain* baselines are compared to our results and to the results reported by (Spitkovsky et al., 2011a). It is obvious, that using the Noun-Root suppression ("Our-NR" column) improves the parsing quality for the majority of languages and has higher scores for 12 (out of 19) languages than previous results ("Spi5" and "Spi6"). If we do not use the Noun-Root suppression ("Our" column), the scores are higher for 6 (7) languages compared to "Spi5" ("Spi6"), but the averaged attachment score is quite similar.

Interestingly, Arabic, Danish, and Japanese have very high *LeftChain* (*RightChain*) baseline and no method was able to beat them so far.

7 Conclusions

We described our novel work on unsupervised dependency parser based on Gibbs sampling. We showed that introducing treeness constraint in sampling improves attachment score for Czech from about 45% to 50%. The other improvement was caused by repressing Noun-Root dependencies. We reached 49.9% unlabeled attachment score for Czech. If we apply the same parser configuration to 19 languages available in the CoNLL 2006 and 2007 data, we outperform the previously published results for 12 languages.

Our method does not work well for English. It reached only 24% UAS, which is far below the *RightChain* baseline. This is the opposite of other approaches (based on DMV), which are very good for English and whose results for other languages

[5]train.conll and test.conll files for CoNLL2006 languages and dtrain.conll and dtest.conll for CoNLL2007 languages.

are presented rarely.

In the future, we would like to add a fertility model and introduce lexicalization. We are also aware that the parsing quality strongly depends on the tag set, so we plan to incorporate some form of unsupervised tagging or word clustering.

Acknowledgement

This research was supported by the grants GA201/09/H057 (Res Informatica), MSM0021620838, GAUK 116310, and by the European Commission's 7th Framework Program (FP7) under grant agreement n° 247762 (FAUST). We thank anonymous reviewers for their valuable comments and suggestions.

References

D. Aldous. 1985. Exchangeability and related topics. In *l'Ecole d'ete de probabilites de Saint-Flour*, pages 1–198, Berlin, Germany. Springer.

Samuel Brody. 2010. It depends on the translation: unsupervised dependency parsing via word alignment. In *Proceedings of the 2010 Conference on Empirical Methods in Natural Language Processing*, EMNLP '10, pages 1214–1222, Stroudsburg, PA, USA. Association for Computational Linguistics.

Peter F. Brown, Vincent J.Della Pietra, Stephen A. Della Pietra, and Robert. L. Mercer. 1993. The Mathematics of Statistical Machine Translation: Parameter Estimation. *Computational Linguistics*, 19:263–311.

Sabine Buchholz and Erwin Marsi. 2006. CoNLL-X shared task on multilingual dependency parsing. In *Proceedings of the Tenth Conference on Computational Natural Language Learning*, CoNLL-X '06, pages 149–164, Stroudsburg, PA, USA. Association for Computational Linguistics.

Y. J. Chu and T. H. Liu. 1965. On the Shortest Arborescence of a Directed Graph. *Science Sinica*, 14:1396–1400.

Shay B. Cohen, Kevin Gimpel, and Noah A. Smith. 2008. Logistic normal priors for unsupervised probabilistic grammar induction. In *Neural Information Processing Systems*, pages 321–328.

W. R. Gilks, S. Richardson, and D. J. Spiegelhalter. 1996. *Markov chain Monte Carlo in practice*. Interdisciplinary statistics. Chapman & Hall.

Jan Hajič et al. 2006. Prague Dependency Treebank 2.0. CD-ROM, Linguistic Data Consortium, LDC Catalog No.: LDC2006T01, Philadelphia.

William P. Headden, III, Mark Johnson, and David McClosky. 2009. Improving unsupervised dependency parsing with richer contexts and smoothing. In *Proceedings of Human Language Technologies: The 2009 Annual Conference of the North American Chapter of the Association for Computational Linguistics*, NAACL '09, pages 101–109, Stroudsburg, PA, USA. Association for Computational Linguistics.

Dan Klein and Christopher D. Manning. 2004. Corpus-based induction of syntactic structure: models of dependency and constituency. In *Proceedings of the 42nd Annual Meeting on Association for Computational Linguistics*, ACL '04, Stroudsburg, PA, USA. Association for Computational Linguistics.

Ryan McDonald, Fernando Pereira, Kiril Ribarov, and Jan Hajič. 2005. Non-Projective Dependency Parsing using Spanning Tree Algorithms. In *Proceedings of Human Langauge Technology Conference and Conference on Empirical Methods in Natural Language Processing (HTL/EMNLP)*, pages 523–530, Vancouver, BC, Canada.

Tahira Naseem and Regina Barzilay. 2011. Using Semantic Cues to Learn Syntax. In *AAAI*.

Joakim Nivre, Johan Hall, Sandra Kübler, Ryan McDonald, Jens Nilsson, Sebastian Riedel, and Deniz Yuret. 2007. The CoNLL 2007 Shared Task on Dependency Parsing. In *Proceedings of the CoNLL Shared Task Session of EMNLP-CoNLL 2007*, pages 915–932, Prague, Czech Republic, June. Association for Computational Linguistics.

Roy Schwartz, Omri Abend, Roi Reichart, and Ari Rappoport. 2011. Neutralizing linguistically problematic annotations in unsupervised dependency parsing evaluation. In *Proceedings of the 49th Annual Meeting of the Association for Computational Linguistics: Human Language Technologies*, pages 663–672, Portland, Oregon, USA, June. Association for Computational Linguistics.

Noah Ashton Smith. 2007. *Novel estimation methods for unsupervised discovery of latent structure in natural language text*. Ph.D. thesis, Baltimore, MD, USA. AAI3240799.

Valentin I. Spitkovsky, Hiyan Alshawi, and Daniel Jurafsky. 2011a. Lateen EM: Unsupervised training with multiple objectives, applied to dependency grammar induction. In *Proceedings of the 2011 Conference on Empirical Methods in Natural Language Processing (EMNLP 2011)*.

Valentin I. Spitkovsky, Hiyan Alshawi, and Daniel Jurafsky. 2011b. Punctuation: Making a point in unsupervised dependency parsing. In *Proceedings of the Fifteenth Conference on Computational Natural Language Learning (CoNLL-2011)*.

Guided Self Training for Sentiment Classification

Brett Drury
LIAAD-INESC
Portugal
brett.drury@gmail.com

Luís Torgo
Fac. Sciences
LIAAD-INESC, Portugal
ltorgo@inescporto.pt

J.J Almedia
Dept. of Engineering
University of Minho, Portugal
jj@di.uminho.pt

Abstract

The application of machine learning techniques to classify text documents into sentiment categories has become an increasingly popular area of research. These techniques rely upon the availability of labelled data, but in certain circumstances the availability of pre-classified documents may be limited. Limited labelled data can impact the performance of the model induced from it. There are a number of strategies which can compensate for the lack of labelled data, however these techniques may be suboptimal if the initial labelled data selection does not contain a sufficient cross section of the total document collection. This paper proposes a variant of self-training as a strategy to this problem. The proposed technique uses a high precision classifier (linguistic rules) to influence the selection of training candidates which are labelled by the base learner in an iterative self-training process. The linguistic knowledge encoded in the high precision classifier corrects high-confidence errors made by the base classifier in a preprocessing step. This step is followed by a standard self training cycle. The technique was evaluated in three domains: user generated reviews for (1) airline meals, (2) university professors and (3) music against: (1) constrained learning strategies (voting and veto), (2) induction and (3) standard self-training. The evaluation measure was by estimated F-Measure. The results demonstrate clear advantage for the proposed method for classifying text documents into sentiment categories in domains where there is limited amounts of training data.

1 Introduction

The application of machine learning techniques to classify text into sentiment categories has become an increasingly popular area of research. Models induced from data can be very accurate(Halevy et al., 2009), but a learner may require a significant amount of data to induce a model which can accurately classify a text collection. Large volumes of labelled documents may not be readily available or may be expensive to obtain. Models induced from small volumes of labelled data may be sub-optimal because the pre-classified data may not contain a sufficient cross-section of the document collection. The field of Semi-Supervised Learning (SSL) offers a number of possible strategies to compensate for the lack of labelled data. These techniques may not be effective if the model induced from the initial set of labelled data is biased or ineffective because these strategies can exacerbate the weaknesses in the initial model. This paper describes a SSL strategy that is a variant of Self-Training (ST). ST is an iterative process that obtains models with increasingly larger samples of labelled data. At each iteration the current model is used to classify the unlabelled data. The observations which the model has a high confidence in the classification are added to the next training sample with the classification of the model as the label.

The evaluation of the effectiveness of our proposal involved the experimental comparison with the following types of methods: (1) constrained, (2) inductive and (3) standard self- training. Training data was randomly selected from the total document collection and ranged from 1% of the total collection to 5%. The F-Measure was estimated by testing the model against the total document collection with the training data removed. The experiments were run 20 times for each training intervals with two separate learners: Naive Bayes and

Language Models. The domains which were evaluated were:(1) airline meals, (2) university teachers and (3) music reviews. The results demonstrate clear advantage for the proposed method for classifying text documents in domains where the models induced from the training data were weak.

1.1 Related Work

There are a number of approaches which use words (Hatzivassiloglou and McKeown, 1997)(Riloff and Weibe, 2003), phrases (Liu, 2007) and grammars (Drury and Almeida, 2011) to classify documents into sentiment categories. Linguistic rules may not be sufficient in domains which have non-standard linguistic features and lexicons. Another approach is to use labelled samples of the domain as training data to construct a classifier. Labelled data can be expensive to obtain. Semi-supervised learning can assist by adding labels to unlabelled data and using them as training data. A sub-field of semi-supervised learning uses constraints to limit the documents selected (Abney, 2007a). For example: co-training uses different views of the same data to train individual classifiers and restraining the documents selected to the documents which are labelled equally by the separate classifiers. The notion of "hard" constraints has been extended to with the idea of "soft" constraints (Druck et al., 2008). Druck (Druck et al., 2008) provides an example of using the Noun, "puck" to identify hockey documents. This type of soft constraint may not be successful with sentiment classification because separate classes can share features because a sentiment word can be negated. For example: the Noun, "recession" could be associated with a negative class, but with the addition of the word "v-shaped" transforms "recession" to a positive feature because the phrase "v-shaped recession" is positive, consequently the addition of the feature "recession" for the negative class would be an error. Chang (wei Chang et al., 2007) proposed the use of constraints to label a pool of unlabelled data and then use that pool of newly labelled data to update the model. Chang's approach would be insufficient for sentiment classification because of shared features where any individual unigram constraints could be negated and the pool of sentiment indicators are very large and that constraining the learner may produce a biased learner.

2 Proposed Strategy

The proposed ST variant - Guided Self-Training (GST) - differs from standard ST in the selection of the examples to add in each iteration. The variation is the use of a high precision classifier (linguistic rules) to select a small number of high confidence candidates ("the high confidence pool"). These rules are used to test the learner against the high confidence pool, and if the learner makes a high confidence erroneous classification of a member of this pool then the member is added to the correct class by the linguistic rules.

This training data is supplemented with extra data which the learner selects with high confidence from both non-members and members of the high confidence pool. The assumption of this proposed method is that the correction of erroneous high confidence classifications improves the performance of a learner and that the amount of improvement is directly related to the number of corrections. The learner is not explicitly constrained and is allowed to learn features from documents which are not in the high confidence pool, but the learner is "guided" to make correct selections when it makes serious errors.

2.1 Motivation

The principal motivation for this work was to identify a strategy which could construct a robust model which could classify documents into sentiment categories. Documents which are used for sentiment classification are often linguistically complex because they can contain: 1. multi word expressions which have semantic idiomaticity and 2. non standard spelling and grammar. These types of domains are difficult to classify because of the aforementioned features and because of the large volume of available documents to classify, for example Twitter claims that there are 50 millions tweets posted in a day[1]. It is not feasible to manually label or construct rules to label a significant number of these tweets. Learners which are constructed from a small subset of data are likely to be weak and traditional SSL techniques may not be suitable.

2.2 Problem Definition

GST is designed to improve the performance of a classifier in domains with the following characteristics:

[1]http://goo.gl/qXldd

Method	Avg. Precision
Method 1	57% (±3)
Method 2	75% (±3)

Table 1: Precision of Classifiers Induced from Rule Selected Data

- Limited amount of labelled data
- Labelling of large amounts of data is not feasible
- External resources such as general sentiment dictionaries (Esuli and Sebastiani, 2006) does not aid sentiment classification

2.3 Selection of high precision rule classifier

There are a number of methodologies to create a rule classifier. The rule classifier for GST must have a high precision and therefore recall was a secondary consideration. Two methodologies were considered: one which considered a sequence of POS tags to create bigrams (method 1) and the other which used manually selected features from training data and expanded them with Wordnet (Fellbaum, 1998) (method 2). These methodologies are described in detail by Liu (Liu, 2007). The competing methods selected and labelled data from reviews for airline food. Method 1 labels a document as according to the average opinion orientation (Liu, 2007). Method 2 labels a document as positive or negative if it has at least a difference of three unigrams from a given class. The difference of three unigrams produces an accurate classifier, but at the expense of recall (Riloff and Weibe, 2003).

The selection of the high precision classifier was by precision score of Language Models induced from the data selected by each competing methodology. A mean average precision score was calculated from a 2 X 5 cross validation process. The results are described in Table 1.

In this context, the GST method will use Method 2[2] to construct a dictionary for the high precision classifier because it has a higher precision than method 1. The rule classifier for GST will classify documents in the same manner as the rule selection test, i.e. review must have at least a difference of three unigrams from a given class. The proposed GST method is not dependent on this rule construction methodology, but any alternative rule classifier must have high precision which is normally at the cost of low recall.

2.4 GST Algorithm

The proposed GST method is described in Algorithm 1. GST takes two main inputs: the labelled (LD) and unlabelled (UD) data sets. The outer loop (lines 3-26) represent the typical self-training iterations. The uniqueness of the proposal are the following:

- Documents classified by the base learner with a high confidence which are contrary to the high precision classification (the pool of high confidence candidates) are assigned to the high precision classification. These documents are assigned to the labelled data for training in the next iteration.
- The high precision classifier can abdicate (i.e no decision) and therefore high confidence candidates can be selected by the base learner with out the explicit agreement of the high precision classifier.

A model is induced from the selected data. At each iteration, weaknesses in the model are corrected, but the document selection is not constrained to the pool of high confidence candidates (high precision classifier classifications), and consequently the learner reaches its optimum performance with less training data than competing methods.

3 Experimental Evaluation

Three domains were chosen for the evaluation of the proposed technique: (1) user generated reviews of airline meals (airlinemeals.net, 2010), (2) user generated reviews of university lecturers (ratemyprofessors.com, 2010) and (3) user generated reviews of music concerts and records (reviewcentre.com, 2010) [11][3]. The domains demonstrated the following linguistic characteristics: (1) invented words, (2) slang, (3) profanity, (4) non standard spelling and grammar, (5) multi-word expressions (MWE) and (6) non standard punctuation.

[2] Method 2 recorded an average precision of 95% and recall of 20% when the rules directly classified candidate data and were allowed to abdicate.

[3] Data and dictionaries can be found at http://goo.gl/IHL6V

Algorithm 1 Description of GST Candidate Selection Cycle

```
procedure GST(LD, UD, sThr, Rules, Learner)
    ▷ LD and UD - The collections of labelled an unlabelled documents, respectively; sThr - The minimum classification confidence for a document to be considered for addition to the labelled training set; Rules - A series of linguistic rules which return a classification for a document; Learner - the classification algorithm that is to be self-trained. CD - a container for a corrected documents - i.e. errors made by the base classifier AD A container for documents where the base and high precision classifier don't disagree TD - a container for documents in CD which are not selected for training

    Model ← Learner(LD)                                   ▷ Learn a classifier
    repeat
        lClass ← Model.classify(UD)
        rClass ← Rules.classify(UD)
        CD ← {}
        AD ← {}
        ▷ Check agreement between Learner and Rules
        for all d ∈ UD do
            if lClass.confidence[d] ≥ sThr then
                UD ← UD \ d
                if rClass[d] ≠ NULL and rClass[d] ≠ lClass[d] then
                    CD ← CD ∪ {< d, rClass[d] >}
                else
                    AD ← AD ∪ {< d, lClass[d] >}
                end if
            end if
        end for
        count ← Count(CD)
        if count == 0 then
            count ← Count(AD)
        end if
        TD ← ReturnRandomDocs(AD, count)
        UD ← UD ∪ (AD \ TD)
        LD ← LD ∪ CD ∪ TD
        Model ← Learner(LD)                               ▷ Get a new model
    until terminationCriterion
    return Model
end procedure
```

3.1 Experimental Setup

Each document contained: the text and a form of rating. The rating was taken as an indication of the polarity of the review. The criteria for class assignment is described in Table 2. Documents not satisfying the criteria for class assignment were removed from our experiments.

These resulting labelled data sets were used to compare:

- Two separate base learners (Naive Bayes and Language Models)

Domain	Positive Category	Negative Category
Airline Meals	4 -5 Stars	1-2 Stars
Teacher Reviews	Good Quality	Poor Quality
Music Reviews	4-5 Stars	1-2 Stars

Table 2: Polarity Criteria

- Alternative strategies

The evaluation was by means of an estimated F-Measure. The experiments used increasing larger random selection of documents as training data. The smallest selection of data was 1% of the total and the largest 5%. The increments were in steps of 1%, for example the second iteration of the experiment was 2%, the third 3% etc. At each iteration the experiment was repeated 20 times, for example the 1st iteration there would be 20 random samples of 1% and 20 estimations of F-Measure. An overview of the process is the following: 1. randomly select training data (the LD set in Algorithm 1) and 2. "artificially unlabel" the remaining documents to create the UD.

The experiments were repeated using Language Models and Naive Bayes Classifier as the baseline classifiers within the GST algorithm.

We have compared our proposed method against three alternative strategies:

(1) inductive, (2) self-training and (3) constrained learning.

- Inductive: An inductive strategy induces a classification model using only the labelled data (Abney, 2007b).

- Self-Training: An iterative process where at each step a model is induced from the current labelled data and it is used to classify the unlabelled data set. The model assigns a "confidence measure" to each classification. If the classification confidence measure is greater than a predefined threshold then the respective unlabelled cases are added to the new iteration training data with the classifier assigned label. At the end of the cycle the learner is trained on the "new labelled data set". This cycle continues until a stopping condition is met (Abney, 2007b). To ensure an equitable comparison the stopping condition for both self-training and GST was 5 iterations.

- Constrained Learning: The alternate constrained learning strategies were Voting and Veto.
  - Voting strategy: Selects documents if both the classifiers agree on the classification of the document
  - Veto strategy: The base learner selects the data, but high precision classifier adds the label, consequently the high precision classifier vetoes a dissenting leaner classification. The high precision classifier is not allowed to abdicate.

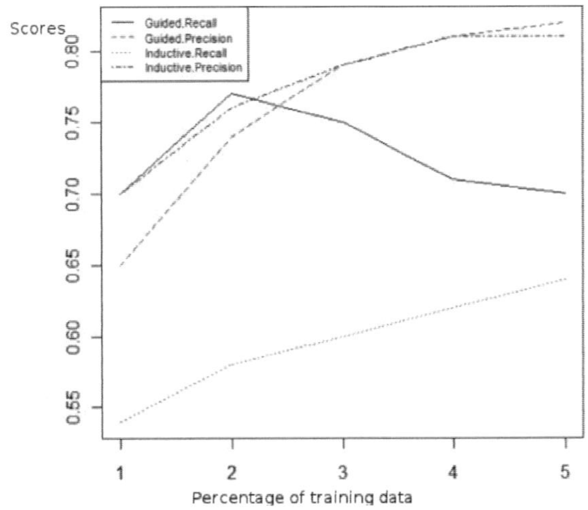

Figure 1: Language Models: Comparative Recall and Precision for Teacher Domain

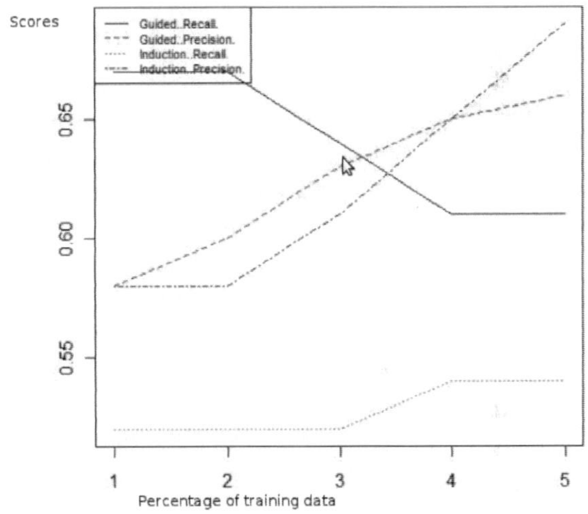

Figure 2: Naive Bayes: Comparative Recall and Precision for Airline Meals Domain

4 Experimental Results

The *Airline Food Domain* results are presented in Table 3. The results demonstrate a clear advantage for the proposed strategy for both classifiers. The results demonstrate a significant gain in F-Measure at the 2% of domain for training for both classifiers. The gain in F-Measure halts at the 3% of domain for training. The two inductive strategies gain F-Measure as training data increases.

The *Teachers Domain* results are presented in Table 4. The results demonstrate a clear advantage

		% of Data for Training				
		1	2	3	4	5
Algorithm	Classifier	F-Measure	F-Measure	F-Measure	F-Measure	F-Measure
Fully Supervised	Naive Bayes	0.91				
Fully Supervised	Language Models	0.98				
GST	Naive Bayes	0.52 ±0.05	0.61 ±0.01	0.63 ±0.01	0.63 ±0.01	0.63 ±0.01
GST	Language Models	0.49 ±0.04	0.60 ±0.02	0.64 ±0.01	0.64 ±0.01	0.63 ±0.02
Voting	Naive Bayes	0.48 ±0.00	0.49 ±0.00	0.50 ±0.01	0.51 ±0.01	0.51 ±0.01
Voting	Language Models	0.48 ±0.00	0.49 ±0.00	0.49 ±0.00	0.50 ±0.00	0.51 ±0.00
Inductive (LD)	Naive Bayes	0.51 ±0.01	0.51 ±0.01	0.52 ±0.01	0.54 ±0.01	0.55 ±0.01
Inductive (LD)	Language Models	0.49 ±0.02	0.50 ±0.01	0.51 ±0.01	0.52 ±0.01	0.53 ±0.01
Inductive (LD+RC)	Naive Bayes	0.54 ±0.00	0.55 ±0.00	0.56 ±0.00	0.56 ±0.00	0.57 ±0.00
Inductive (LD+RC)	Language Models	0.53 ±0.00	0.54 ±0.00	0.55 ±0.00	0.55 ±0.00	0.56 ±0.00
Self-Training (LD)	Naive Bayes	0.50 ±0.01	0.50 ±0.01	0.51 ±0.01	0.51 ±0.01	0.52 ±0.01
Self-Training (LD)	Language Models	0.48 ±0.01	0.49 ±0.00	0.50 ±0.00	0.50 ±0.01	0.51 ±0.00
Veto	Naive Bayes	0.54 ±0.00	0.55 ±0.00	0.56 ±0.00	0.49 ±0.00	0.49 ±0.00
Veto	Language Models	0.53 ±0.00	0.54 ±0.00	0.55 ±0.00	0.55 ±0.00	0.56 ±0.00

Table 3: Airline Meals Experimental Results

for the proposed strategy. In common with the airline food domain the Guided Self-Training(GST) shows a large gain in F-Measure at 2% of domain for training. The gain in F-Measure is more pronounced for language models. GST demonstrates a reduction in F-Measure with further increases in training data. The reduction in F-Measure is within the mean standard deviation. The inductive strategists in common with the airline food domain gains F-Measure with increases in training data. The self-training strategy gains in F-Measure increase with training data, but at a faster rate than the inductive strategies. The voting schemes also demonstrate a gain in F-Measure, but at a lower rate than the inductive and self-training strategies.

The *Music Review Domain* results are presented in Table 4. The results demonstrates that the proposed strategy does not show any distinct advantage over the competing strategies. The models induced from the labelled data seem robust and the various SSL strategies fail to improve this strategy.

4.1 Discussion of Results

Strategies which have access to rule selected data frequently have a higher precision measure, but this improvement is frequently at the cost of lower recall. For example the mean average recall and precision for the voting strategy in the Airline Food domain was 0.5 and 0.7, where as the inductive strategy yielded recall and precision of: 0.51 and 0.62. A possible explanation for this phenomenon is that fact that the high precision classifier may only classify a very specific sample of documents. The addition of these documents labelled by the high precision classifier to the initial data set of the models we could be biasing the classifier towards learning very specific rules, which may negatively impact on recall, but may boost precision. The GST method does not suffer from a decrease in recall. A possible explanation could be the high precision classifier is being used with a different purpose within GST when compared to the (LD+RC) learners. In GST high precision classifier are used to supervise the classifications of a standard base learner with the goal of avoiding very obvious mistakes. In the (LD+RC) learners the rules are used to add more labelled data to the training set available to the learners. These are two different uses of the high precision classifier and our experiments clearly provide evidence towards the advantage of our proposal. In effect, GST improvement in precision is not offset by a drop in recall.

The graphs illustrated in Figure 2 and Figure 1 provide a comparative analysis of the precision and recall for the inductive and proposed strategy in the airline and teacher domains respectively. These graphs provide some evidence for the assertion that the F-Measure gains are at not at the expense of a drop in recall because until 2% domain training data there are gains in precision and no drop in recall. The airline domain demonstrates a gain in recall. The recall drops from 2% onwards, however recall is always significantly higher than the recall for the inductive strategy. The GST strategy continues to gain precision with increases in training data.

4.2 Discussion of Methodology

The assumption of the GST methodology is that correcting high confidence erroneous classifications and including the documents as training

	% of Data for Training					
		1	2	3	4	5
Algorithm	Classifier	F-Measure	F-Measure	F-Measure	F-Measure	F-Measure
Fully Supervised	Naive Bayes	0.96				
Fully Supervised	Language Models	0.99				
GST	Naive Bayes	0.67 ±0.04	0.71 ±0.02	0.67 ±0.03	0.66 ±0.02	0.65 ±0.02
GST	Language Models	0.58 ±0.01	0.75 ±0.01	0.76 ±0.01	0.74 ±0.02	0.73 ±0.02
Voting	Naive Bayes	0.47 ±0.01	0.48 ±0.01	0.51 ±0.01	0.52 ±0.01	0.54 ±0.01
Voting	Language Models	0.45 ±0.01	0.48 ±0.01	0.49 ±0.01	0.51 ±0.01	0.53 ±0.01
Inductive (LD)	Naive Bayes	0.56 ±0.03	0.60 ±0.02	0.63 ±0.03	0.65 ±0.02	0.66 ±0.02
Inductive (LD)	Language Models	0.52 ±0.02	0.59 ±0.03	0.61 ±0.02	0.64 ±0.02	0.66 ±0.02
Inductive (LD+RC)	Naive Bayes	0.53 ±0.00	0.54 ±0.00	0.54 ±0.05	0.57 ±0.00	0.58 ±0.00
Inductive (LD+RC)	Language Models	0.52 ±0.00	0.53 ±0.00	0.55 ±0.00	0.56 ±0.00	0.57 ±0.00
Self-Training (LD)	Naive Bayes	0.53 ±0.03	0.56 ±0.02	0.60 ±0.02	0.62 ±0.03	0.64 ±0.02
Self-Training (LD)	Language Models	0.49 ±0.02	0.55 ±0.03	0.57 ±0.02	0.60 ±0.02	0.62 ±0.02
Veto	Naive Bayes	0.52 ±0.00	0.54 ±0.00	0.55 ±0.00	0.57 ±0.00	0.58 ±0.00
Veto	Language Models	0.52 ±0.00	0.53 ±0.00	0.55 ±0.00	0.56 ±0.00	0.57 ±0.00

Table 4: Teacher Review Experimental Results

	% of Data for Training					
		1	2	3	4	5
Algorithm	Classifier	F-Measure	F-Measure	F-Measure	F-Measure	F-Measure
Fully Supervised	Naive Bayes	0.96				
Fully Supervised	Language Models	0.99				
GST	Naive Bayes	0.51 ±0.01	0.46 ±0.02	0.48 ±0.02	0.49 ±0.02	0.50 ±0.03
GST	Language Models	0.54 ±0.01	0.55 ±0.01	0.49 ±0.01	0.49 ±0.02	0.48 ±0.02
Voting	Naive Bayes	0.43 ±0.00	0.44 ±0.00	0.45 ±0.01	0.46 ±0.01	0.47 ±0.01
Voting	Language Models	0.43 ±0.00	0.45 ±0.01	0.45 ±0.01	0.46 ±0.01	0.47 ±0.01
Inductive (LD)	Naive Bayes	0.57 ±0.09	0.64 ±0.07	0.61 ±0.07	0.66 ±0.07	0.65 ±0.06
Inductive (LD)	Language Models	0.54 ±0.09	0.59 ±0.11	0.60 ±0.07	0.65 ±0.08	0.67 ±0.06
Inductive (LD+RC)	Naive Bayes	0.45 ±0.00	0.45 ±0.00	0.46 ±0.01	0.47 ±0.01	0.48 ±0.01
Inductive (LD+RC)	Language Models	0.45 ±0.01	0.46 ±0.00	0.46 ±0.00	0.47 ±0.00	0.48 ±0.01
Self-Training (LD)	Naive Bayes	0.58 ±0.01	0.64 ±0.07	0.61 ±0.07	0.66 ±0.08	0.65 ±0.06
Self-Training (LD)	Language Models	0.54 ±0.09	0.58 ±0.12	0.60 ±0.08	0.65 ±0.09	0.66 ±0.07
Veto	Naive Bayes	0.45 ±0.00	0.45 ±0.00	0.46 ±0.01	0.47 ±0.01	0.48 ±0.01
Veto	Language Models	0.45 ±0.00	0.46 ±0.01	0.46 ±0.00	0.47 ±0.00	0.48 ±0.01

Table 5: Music Reviews Experimental Results

data will improve the performance of the induced model. An experiment was conducted where the number of documents corrected was recorded per training cycle. The experiment was conducted for the 1% of domain for training. The results are described in Figure 3. The two domains in which GST gained the highest F-Measure there is a high level of corrections in the first training cycle. The remaining cycles show a small number of corrections. The music domain demonstrates a small number of corrections and may account for the relatively poor performance of GST in this domain.

The second assumption of this methodology is that the classifier which corrects the erroneous classifications must be accurate and that classifiers with lower precision will effect the performance of the GST strategy. A further experiment was conducted with a high precision classifier which was constructed with a lower precision methodology (method 1). The experiment was conducted on the airline meals domain data. The results are presented in Table 6. The results were the worst of all of the strategies tested. The lower precision classifier "modified" correct high confidence classifications made by the base learner rather than the high confidence erroneous classifications. The "erroneous corrections" inhibited the base learner and induced a weak model. Although the aforementioned methodology had an inferior precision than the classifier used for the proposed strategy its overall performance was slightly better. Table 6 shows the inductive(RD+LC) strategy which used rule selected data gained a slightly higher F-Measure than for the inductive(RD+LC) strategy in the main experiments (Table 3).

5 Conclusion

This paper describes a new semi-supervised classification method for sentiment classification (GST) designed with the goal of handling document clas-

		% of Data for Training				
		1	2	3	4	5
Algorithm	Classifier	F-Measure	F-Measure	F-Measure	F-Measure	F-Measure
GST	Language Models	0.13 ±0.00	0.15 ±0.00	0.17 ±0.00	0.21 ±0.00	0.25 ±0.00
Inductive (RD+LC)	Language Models	0.58 ±0.00	0.58 ±0.00	0.59 ±0.00	0.59 ±0.00	0.59 ±0.00

Table 6: GST Strategy with lower precision classifier

sification tasks where there are limited labelled documents. The proposed technique can perform well in circumstances where more mature strategies may perform poorly. The characteristics of the domains where it is thought that this strategy will offer a clear advantage are the following: (1) model induced from labelled data makes obvious mistakes, (2) adding more data (either manually or by rules) does not improve performance, and (3) it is possible to construct a high precision rule based classifier. GST uses linguistic information encoded into a high precision classifier. This information is not added on mass where the learner may be biased towards information captured by the high precision classifier, but it is added in areas where the learner is weak. GST also selects a larger variety of documents than the high precision classifier because the base learner self-selects high confidence candidates from the unlabelled data. The constant testing of the learner prevents drift which may occur in classical self-training. The proposed technique provides a viable alternative to current semi-supervised classification strategies, as our experimental results demonstrate.

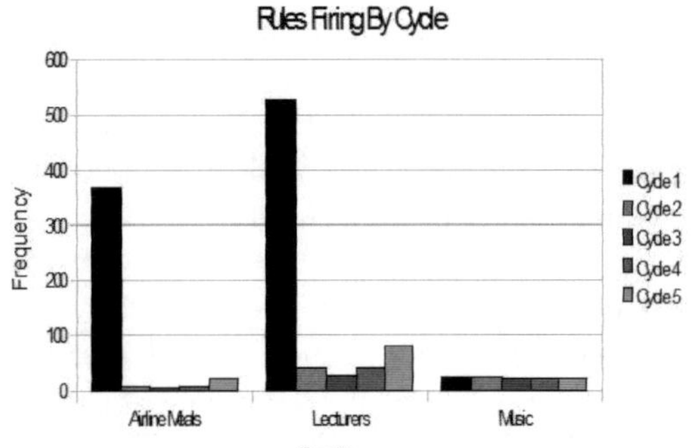

Figure 3: No. Corrected Documents Per Training Cycle.

References

S. Abney. 2007a. *Semisupervised Learning for Computational Linguistics*. Chapman & Hall/CRC. Chapter 9: Agreement Constraints.

S. Abney. 2007b. *Semisupervised Learning for Computational Linguistics*. Chapman & Hall/CRC. Chapter two: Self Training and Co-Training.

airlinemeals.net. 2010. Airlinemeals. `http://www.airlinemeals.net/`, consulted in 2010.

Gregory Druck, Gideon S. Mann, and Andrew Mccallum. 2008. Learning from labeled features using generalized expectation criteria. In *Research and Development in Information Retrieval*, pages 595–602.

Brett Drury and José João Almeida. 2011. Identification of fine grained feature based event and sentiment phrases from business news stories. In *WIMS*, page 27.

A. Esuli and F. Sebastiani. 2006. Sentiwordnet: A publicly available lexical resource for opinion mining. In *In Proceedings of the 5th Conference on Language Resources and Evaluation (LREC 06*, pages 417 – 422.

C. Fellbaum. 1998. *WordNet: An Electronical Lexical Database*. The MIT Press, Cambridge, MA.

Alon Halevy, Peter Norvig, and Fernando Pereira. 2009. The unreasonable effectiveness of data. *IEEE Intelligent Systems*, 2:8–12.

Vasileios Hatzivassiloglou and Kathleen R. McKeown. 1997. Predicting the semantic orientation of adjectives. In *Proceedings of the eighth conference on European chapter of the Association for Computational Linguistics*, pages 174–181.

Bing Liu. 2007. *Web Data Mining: chapter(Opinion Mining)*. Springer.

ratemyprofessors.com. 2010. Ratemyprofessors. `http://www.ratemyprofessors.com/`, consulted in 2010.

reviewcentre.com. 2010. Reviewcentre. `http://www.reviewcentre.com/`, consulted in 2010.

E. Riloff and J. Weibe. 2003. Learning extraction patterns for subjective expressions. In *In Proceedings of the 2003 Conference on Empirical Methods in Natural Language Processing*, pages 105–112.

Ming wei Chang, Lev Ratinov, and Dan Roth. 2007. Guiding semi-supervision with constraint-driven learning. In *In Proc. of the Annual Meeting of the ACL*.

Investigating the Applicability of current Machine-Learning based Subjectivity Detection Algorithms on German Texts

Malik Atalla
Technische Universität Berlin
atalla@cs.tu-berlin.de,

Christian Scheel and **Ernesto William De Luca** and **Sahin Albayrak**
DAI-Labor, Technische Universität Berlin
{christian.scheel,ernesto.deluca,sahin.albayrak}@dai-labor.de

Abstract

In the field of subjectivity detection, algorithms automatically classify pieces of text into fact or opinion. Many different approaches have been successfully evaluated on English or Chinese texts. Nevertheless the assumption that these algorithms equally perform on all other languages cannot be verified yet. It is our intention to encourage more research in other languages, making a start with German. Therefore, this work introduces a German corpus for subjectivity detection on German news articles. We carry out this study in which we choose a number of state of the art subjectivity detection approaches and implement them. Finally we show and compare these algorithms' performances and give advice on how to use and extend the introduced dataset.

1 Introduction

The detection of subjective statements in natural language texts is necessary for the analysis of opinions and the extraction of facts for knowledge retrieval. The continuously increasing number of natural language texts on the Internet and the need for opinion detection and fact retrieval makes research on subjectivity detection more and more important.

The economic impact is rising just as much. The Internet has long turned into an open platform in which everybody can participate and contribute his or her share of opinions.

Subjectivity detection also affects upcoming fields of research like knowledge retrieval. Crawlers have to distinguish between objective and subjective texts in order to extract given facts only from the objective parts.

The other way round, in the field of opinion analysis, many approaches are supposed to be applied on subjective texts. In *polarity classification* pieces of text are classified into complementary viewpoints. In this field of research facts are considered noise to the problem. So, finding the subjective parts beforehand can increase the accuracy of such a classifier (Pang and Lee, 2004). Subjectivity detection can support *question-answering systems*. The knowledge about the subjectivity of sentences and sections is important, especially for complex questions that cannot be answered with a single fact, but should rather treat different viewpoints on an issue. Also, subjectivity detection can be useful for *text summarization* which may want to list facts separately from different viewpoints.

In conclusion it can be stated that subjectivity detection is one of the most important preprocessing steps for many IR applications. Such pre-processing has to be language independent or at least the drawbacks for each language have to be known. Hence, the overall goal of this work is to investigate the differences in subjectivity detection in different languages, starting with German and English.

In this work we evaluate a number of machine learning based subjectivity detection approaches on German news texts and on the MPQA corpus, which is the current English standard corpus for subjectivity annotations. We focus on supervised learning approaches for sentence-wise binary classification between subjective and non-subjective sentences without polarity.

After giving an overview over the state of the art in subjectivity detection, we provide details about the MPQA corpus. Afterwards we introduce the *Subjectivity in News Corpus (SNC)*, which was created in the course of this work. The corpus, precisely the German part of the corpus, was annotated in such a way that it provides maximum compatibility with MPQA. Evaluation results on both corpora are compared to conclude if current machine learning based subjectivity detection approaches are equally applicable on both languages. In the concluding part of this work we show which features and ideas are better fit to detect subjectivity in which language and give advice on how to handle subjectivity detection on German texts.

2 Related Work

The field of subjectivity detection can be roughly divided into lexical approaches and machine learning approaches. The lexical approaches are those that incorporate some sort of annotated dictionary. The machine learning approaches represent statements as feature vectors in order to learn to distinguish between subjective and objective statements. In this work, we decided to focus only on supervised learning approaches, which are reviewed in the remainder of this section. In the course of this work a new corpus was created. Therefore this section is completed by a description of corpora for subjectivity detection.

2.1 Subjectivity Detection

Yu and Hatzivassiloglou (2003) presented the first fully supervised machine learning approach in the field of subjectivity detection. As training data a set of Wall Street Journal (WSJ) articles with attached categories is used. In this work the use of a Naive Bayes classifier to distinguish subjective and objective texts has been proposed. These texts were represented by features like extracted unigrams, bigrams, trigrams and POS-tags.

The latter approach does not take the context of a sentence into account. A sentence is more likely to be subjective if the neighboring sentences are subjective as well. Pang and Lee try to tackle this issue with their minimum cut approach (Pang and Lee, 2004). They propose a similar machine learning approach, but additionally assign an association value for each pair of sentences, which is based on the distance of the two sentences in the text. This value encourages the classifier to assign the same label for sentences with a small distance. The structure of the article including the predictions and association values about the sentences are represented by a graph and the final classification is determined by a minimum-cut algorithm.

Wiebe et al. investigate another promising feature in (Wiebe et al., 2004), namely the one of "unique words". It is shown that "apparently, people are creative when they are being opinionated". Note, that this work is a statistical study, where this idea was not carried on as an additional feature in a classifier. The study is based on a corpus of WSJ articles. It is argued that rare words are more likely to occur in opinionated pieces than in objective texts.

Another problem in subjectivity detection and opinion mining in general is the domain and context dependency of many words. It is true in many cases that a word can express an opinion in some context, but be perfectly neutral in another. In their entry for the 2006 Blog Trec, Yang et al. present an approach to this problem (Yang et al., 2006). They use two different sets of training data. One of them contains text about movies, the other about electronic devices. A classifier is trained with each of these data sets and only those features that were useful in both cases are extracted and used in the final classifier. Their rationale is to achieve a feature set that only contains domain-independent features.

Another approach at domain-dependency has been presented by Das and Bandyopadhyay (2009). Instead of discarding domain-dependent words, which could decrease recall, it is tried to determine the topic of a text and use it as a feature in their classifier. Therefore, an additional preprocessing step has been introduced, clustering the training data to determine all possible topics. It is claimed that this feature increases the performance on the MPQA corpus by 2.5%.

Another interesting feature has been proposed in the approach by Chen et al. (2007), where so-called long-distance-bigrams are introduced. Long-distance-bigrams are bigrams which are not consisting of neighboring terms, but of pairs of terms with a certain, fixed distance. 1-distance bigrams would be the same as regular bigrams, 2-distance bigrams have one term in between and so forth. They report a slightly better classification result using a feature set consisting of unigrams, bigrams and 2-distance bigrams, than by just using unigrams. This is interesting in the context of Pang et al. (2002) reporting that using only unigrams performs better than using a combination of unigram and n-gram features.

Banea et al. (2008) wondered if the large amount of NLP tools that already exist for English texts can be exploited for other languages and presented an approach based on machine translation. Different experiments are carried out with

English data and data that was automatically translated into Romanian. Machine translated data is either used as training or as test data. Encouraging results are achieved and it is claimed that machine translation is a viable alternative to creating resources and tools for subjectivity detection in other languages.

2.2 Subjectivity Annotated Corpora

For the English language there are currently two major corpora with subjectivity annotations. The first corpus is the movie data corpus presented in (Pang and Lee, 2004). It contains 5000 subjective and 5000 objective sentences, which have been automatically collected. The subjective sentences are extracted from movie reviews from rottentomatoes.com and the objective ones are from plot summaries from imdb.com. One drawback of this corpus is that it does not contain articles, but only a list of sentences without context.

The second corpus is the MPQA corpus[1], which is a 16000-sentence corpus made up of news articles which are tagged with a complex set of subjectivity annotations. The annotations not only mark subjective statements, but also their polarity, intensity, speaker and other things. Based on these fine-grained annotations the subjectivity of each sentence can be determined. The researchers consider a sentence to be subjective if it contains a *private state*, a subjective *speech event* or an *expressive subjective element*. Otherwise the sentence is objective (Wiebe, 2002). With the term *private state*, they refer to the definition by Quirk et al. (Quirk, 1985) which, according to them, includes mental or emotional states such as opinions, beliefs, thoughts, feelings, emotions, goals, evaluations and judgments.

A speech event refers to a speaking event, such as direct or indirect speech. Speech events are not automatically considered subjective. They can be objective if the credibility of the source is not in doubt and their content is portrayed as fact. The term *expressive subjective element* is based on a publication by Banfield (1982). It is to be used for statements that *"express private states, but do not explicitly state or describe the private state"*.

3 Settings

In this section we first introduce the Subjectivity in News Corpus (SNC), a set of corpora for subjectivity detection. The German part of this corpus, namely *SNC.de*, which was created for this work, is based on German news. *SNC.de* marks the first corpus in a line of upcoming similar corpora for additional languages to be created in the near future. In the second part of this section, we present selected state of the art approaches. The evaluation results of these approaches will provide the baseline for future approaches.

3.1 Structure of the SNC Corpus

Although the introduced corpus will be a multi lingual corpus, the descriptions in this section focus on the German part (SNC.de). In order to be able to evaluate the approaches on German texts, we created an annotated, German corpus. The objective was to provide maximum compatibility with the MPQA corpus. So we abided by the annotation manual as closely as possible and also chose the topics for the texts similarly. Just like in the MPQA corpus, the articles in our corpus are ordered by topic. If we wanted to be completely consistent with MPQA we should also apply the same annotation set. The problem was that many of the very detailed annotations were of no relevance to this work. So we decided to only make binary, sentence-wise annotations, based on the definition of sentence subjectivity presented in (Riloff et al., 2003).

The corpus annotation was carried out by a single annotator using the graphical interface of the GATE[2] tool. So the entire corpus is saved in GATE's own xml serialization format. The annotator attached to each sentence one of the annotations "subjective" or "non-subjective". Suggestions for sentence splitting were provided by the user interface to speed up the annotation process. The annotated texts were saved as entire articles, in order to preserve the context of each sentence. The articles to annotate were randomly chosen from current world news in German.

A comparison of the SNC corpus and the MPQA corpus is given in Table 1.

3.2 Selected Approaches

In this part we list the approaches selected for evaluation and explain why they have been chosen.

Unique Words The feature of unique words, investigated by Wiebe et al. (2004), has never been tried out in a classifier. So, we will use a counter

[1]Referring to version 2.0 in all explanations.

[2]http://gate.ac.uk/

Table 1: Text Statistics about the Corpora.
c: characters; s: sentences; a: article

	SNC	MPQA
Article Statistics		
a in the corpus	278	692
Avrg. a length in s	24,6	22,8
Std.-dev. a lengths	14,3	27,1
Shortest a in s	3	2
Longest a in s	80	275
Sentence Statistics		
s in the corpus	6848	15802
Subjective s	3458	7675
Objective s	3390	8127
Avrg. s length c	124,9	132,4
Std.-Dev. s lengths	67,0	80,1
Same annot. as neighbors	52,0%	59,1%
Avrg. length subj. s in c	133,0	150,1
Avrg. length obj. s in c	116,6	115,0
Word Statistics		
tokens in the corpus	141144	403116
words in the corpus	120128	342165
distinct word forms	18968	22736

for infrequent words in our classifier and evaluate if it contributes to the separation of the two classes. We can use the Leipzig Corpora Collection (LCC)[3] and the BNC to figure out which words of each language classify as rare. We decided to define a rare word form, as one that is not one of the 600.000 most frequent word forms in its language.

POS-Trigrams Santini's approach for genre detection (Santini, 2004) has not yet been picked up by researchers from subjectivity detection. The main idea is to use trigrams of POS-tags as features. We limit the number of features by taking the most frequent POS-trigrams and varying the maximum number.

Unigrams, Bigrams, Trigrams and POS-Tags The machine learning approach by Yu and Hatzivassiloglou (2003) can be considered a standard for later approaches. Sentences are represented by a feature vector which is taken to train a model for separating objective from subjective sentences. A Naive Bayes classifier is used and the feature vector contains unigrams, bigrams, trigrams and POS-tags.

[3]http://corpora.informatik.uni-leipzig.de/download.html

Minimum-Cut Classifier Pang et al. presented the first idea to incorporate context into the classification decision (Pang and Lee, 2004). This classifier is not only based on the content of a sentence, but also on its neighboring sentences.

Long-Distance-Bigrams Chen et al. (2007) proposed the feature of long-distance-bigrams which is a novel idea and therefore worth investigating.

Machine-Translation of Training Data This work aims to investigate if a separate research effort is necessary for every language, or if the existing tools of the English language can be exploited for other languages with acceptable accuracy. Just like in the publication of Banea et al. (2008) we will automatically translate the MPQA corpus, in our case into German, and use it as training or test data. We denote the translation MPQA-G.

4 Experimental Results

Experiments were performed according to selected approaches of Section 3.2. For the experiments with SVMs we chose a linear SVM and used the implementation of Libsvm[4]. For the Naive Bayes classifier the weka[5] implementation was used. The Minimum-Cut classifier was implemented by ourselves based on the description in the publication. For the creation and manipulation of graphs we used the JUNG[6] API.

For the features of the **baseline classifier** we chose POS-tags and a limited number of the most frequent unigrams of the training corpus. It is a simple feature set which nevertheless performs strongly compared to other approaches. We carried out a number of experiments with a Naive Bayes classifier and an SVM and a variable number of unigrams as shown in Fig. 1a. It can be observed that the SVM on the English corpus is rising slightly more steeply than the SVM on the German corpus. This indicates that large numbers of unigrams are more useful for English texts than for German ones.

For the following experiments, the baseline classifier shall be the one using 1500 unigrams. This number seems a reasonable trade-off between computational cost and accuracy.

[4]www.csie.ntu.edu.tw/~cjlin/libsvm/
[5]www.cs.waikato.ac.nz/ml/weka/
[6]http://jung.sourceforge.net/

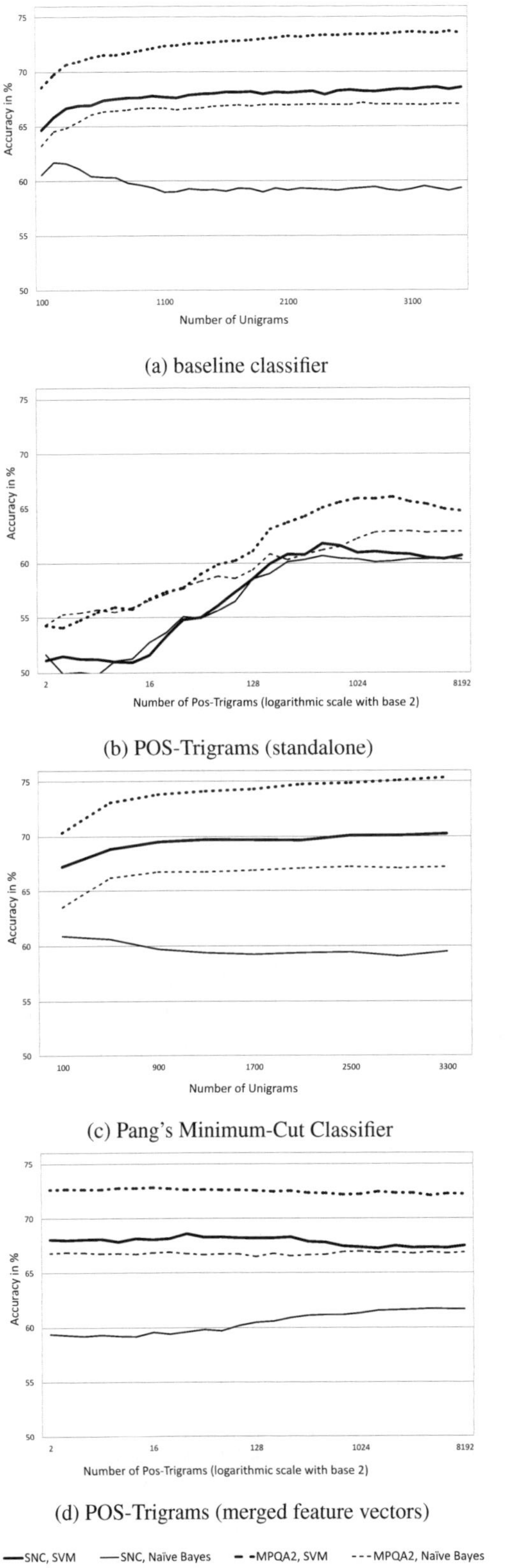

Figure 1: Comparing four approaches for different languages (a–d). Evaluations were performed on the English corpus MPQA and the German corpus SNC.

For every approach where it is applicable we carry out two types of experiments. The first type we would like to call the standalone experiment, in which we use exactly the feature vector described for the approach. The second experiment, the merged-feature-vector-experiment, is done by merging the feature set of our baseline classifier with that of the approach. The second experiment allows us to evaluate if an approach can improve a simple but effective classifier. This is important because some approaches may not be intended as full-blown classifiers, but rather as additional ideas to existing classifiers.

All experiments were carried out by 5-fold cross validation, except some of the experiments with machine-translated data, which is explained separately in the respective section. In all tables the column denotes the corpus used for the cross-validation and the row denotes the experiment's setting, i.e. feature set and classifier. Most experiments are compared to the results of the baseline classifier and to the corpus baseline. The latter is the percentage of the label that occurs more often in the corpus.

4.1 Unique Words

Table 2: Unique Words Feature Experiments. UW: Unique Words; BUW: Base+Unique Words

	SNC	MPQA
Corpus Baseline	*50,50*	*51,40*
UW Training Set (NB)	49,46	51,24
UW Training Set (SVM)	50,76	51,10
UW Statistics (NB)	49,72	51,79
UW Statistics (SVM)	49,31	49,26
UW Tr.+Stats (NB)	48,01	51,65
UW Tr.+Stats (SVM)	53,79	49,81
Baseline Classifier (NB)	*59,21*	*66,84*
Baseline Classifier (SVM)	*67,99*	*72,72*
BUW Training (NB)	59,22	65,87
BUW Training (SVM)	67,76	72,20
BUW Statistics (NB)	59,18	66,80
BUW Statistics (SVM)	68,06	72,68
BUW Tr.+Stats (NB)	59,20	65,99
BUW Tr.+Stats (SVM)	67,91	72,68

For both experiment settings, the standalone setting and the merged-feature-vector setting, we carried out three variants with different features. In the first variant we used a counter for words, that are unique in the scope of the training data, in the second one a counter for words unique according to statistics about the BNC or the LCC and thirdly a feature vector with both of the latter features (see Table 2).

The standalone setting of the unique words feature is not a serious attempt at a classifier. It contains only one or two attributes which is obviously not enough to separate the classes. But we can compare them to the corpus baselines to determine if the features contain any useful information.

Contrary to the claim made in (Wiebe et al., 2004), our experiments could not verify that unique words are a useful feature to detect subjectivity. Using only unique words results in accuracies very close to 50%, except for one setting, but the success for that setting could not be repeated when applying unique words additionally to baseline features. Since the feature does not seem to be useful for either language, no difference could be detected between them.

4.2 POS-Trigrams

When using only trigrams of POS-tags (Fig. 1b), most of the experiments stay far behind their respective baseline classifiers. The only classifier that reaches above the baseline classifier is NB on the German corpus, but only by a small margin.

The standalone experiments indicate that the POS-trigram approach is more useful for German texts than for English ones, when the baseline classifier is taken as comparison value. The best value from the German SVM is slightly closer to the baseline than the best value of the English SVM and for the NB classifiers it is even clearer. The German NB performs better than baseline and the English one significantly worse.

The chart about the experiments with the merged feature vectors (Fig. 1d) illustrates that all results are almost identical to the respective baseline result. Both the English classifiers and the German SVM perform exactly like the baseline classifier in all experiments. This indicates that the POS-trigrams do not contain much useful information that is not already contained in the baseline features. The only exception is again the Naive Bayes classifier applied on the German corpus, which considerably exceeds the baseline classifier's accuracy. The diagram does not show a clear difference between the languages, but it does indicate that POS-trigrams are more useful for German with a classifier on the German corpus being the only one above baseline.

4.3 Unigrams, Bigrams, Trigrams and POS-Tags

Table 3: Experiments with Unigrams, Bigrams, Trigrams and POS-Tags

	SNC	MPQA
Baseline Classifier (NB)	*59,21*	*66,84*
Baseline Classifier (SVM)	*67,99*	*72,72*
Naive Bayes	59,68	66,92
SVM	69,80	74,24

This experiment is carried out with feature vectors containing all unigrams, bigrams, trigrams and POS-tags that occur in the training data, which amounts to a very long vector. The setting with merged feature vectors is not applicable for this experiment because the feature set is a superset of the baseline classifier's feature set.

Table 3 shows that the SVM performs clearly better than the baseline classifier for both corpora, unlike the Naive Bayes classifier which does not show any improvement. The approach is based on a huge amount of different features. The SVM is able to handle this number of features better than the Naive Bayes classifier. Since the features also contain a large amount of redundant data, the Naive Bayes classifier does not perform as well.

For both languages the classifiers achieve about the same distance from the baseline classifiers, namely roughly 2%. So it appears that there is no language dependence for this feature set, but in fact it is much harder to achieve an improvement of 2% when starting from a higher baseline. So, the fact that the distances to the baselines are equal might actually be an indication that the approach is more useful for the English corpus.

4.4 Minimum-Cut Classifier

Fig. 1c shows the results of the experiments with our native implementation of the minimum-cut classifier. The feature set we used is the same as in the baseline classifier. The parameter c, which determines how much influence the context of a sentence has on its classification, was set to the value determined in a parameter optimization. The values are different for SVM (2^{-3}) and Naive Bayes ($2^{-1.9}$). It can be seen that when the SVM is used as base-predictor by the minimum-cut classifier, the accuracy is well above the one of the baseline classifier, but when Naive Bayes is used, the accuracy increased only minimally.

With respect to the difference between the two languages, there is certainly none for the Naive Bayes classifiers. But for the SVMs it seems that the classifier for the German corpus achieves a bigger distance to its baseline classifier than the classifier for the English corpus. The average distances to the baseline classifiers are 1.85% and 1.64% respectively. This might signify that the approach is better fit for German texts, but the reason for the difference might also be that the English baseline classifier is much better in the first place and there is not as much room for improvement as for the German baseline classifier.

4.5 Long-Distance Bigrams

Table 4: Long-Distance Bigrams Experiments; (DB: Distance Bigrams)

	SNC	MPQA
Corpus Baseline	*50,50*	*51,40*
2-DB (NB)	55,55	60,57
2-DB (SVM)	60,29	66,74
2+3-DB (NB)	56,16	61,11
2+3-DB (SVM)	60,63	66,51
2+3+4-DB (NB)	56,20	61,22
2+3+4-DB (SVM)	60,41	66,08
Baseline Classifier (NB)	*59,21*	*66,84*
Baseline Classifier (SVM)	*67,99*	*72,72*
Base+2-DB (NB)	59,67	65,91
Base+2-DB (SVM)	67,59	72,78
Base+2+3-DB (NB)	61,06	66,11
Base+2+3-DB (SVM)	67,29	72,34
Base+2+3+4-DB (NB)	61,63	66,11
Base+2+3+4-DB (SVM)	66,65	72,05

Table 4 shows the results of using only long-distance-bigrams as features. The types of experiments we carried out are similar to those in described in (Chen et al., 2007). First we used only 2-distance-bigrams as features. Then we extended the feature set by adding 3- and 4-distance-bigrams.

All SVMs perform much worse than the baseline classifiers and their distance to that value is about the same for all settings and corpora. Naive Bayes also performs worse than baseline, but a difference between the English and German corpus can be observed. For the German corpus the distances to the baseline classifier are between 3% and 4%, whereas for the English corpora the distance is between 5% and 6%. This observation is affirmed when we apply long-distance-bigrams together with the baseline features.

4.6 Corpus Translation

Table 5: Machine-Translated Data Experiments.

	MPQA-G	*SNC CV*
Baseline Class. (NB)	57,70	*59,21*
Baseline Class. (SVM)	63,43	*67,99*
Base+Most Freq. (NB)	59,80	*60,05*
Base+Most Freq. (SVM)	61,34	*64,22*
POS-Tri 2048 (NB)	57,83	*60,18*
POS-Tri 2048 (SVM)	58,56	*60,88*
Uni+Bi+Tri+POS (NB)	56,31	*59,68*
Uni+Bi+Tri+POS (SVM)	63,52	*69,80*
Baseline (MinCut-NB)	57,71	*59,24*
Baseline (MinCut-SVM)	63,41	*69,68*

Banea et al. proposed machine translation as a way of saving the effort to create NLP tools in languages other than English. Our experiments with machine translated data are shown in Table 5. The middle column shows the results for using our translation of the MPQA corpus (MPQA-G) as training data and SNC as test data. The right column gives the upper bounds of accuracy that can be achieved, which we determined by cross validation on the test data.

It can be seen in many of the settings that the translation approach comes rather close to its upper bound. For many settings the difference is only 2%. We have to acknowledge though, that exactly for those settings where the upper bound is high, the distance to the upper bound is also pretty large. There are three settings with 68% and almost 70% accuracy in CV, but using the translated corpus for training achieves only 63,5% in all of these settings. That means the highest accuracy of the translation approach is significantly lower than the highest cross validation on the test data.

5 Conclusion

While searching for the best machine learning approach for subjectivity detection on multi-lingual texts, we have observed several differences concerning the quality of subjectivity detection in different languages. These differences depend on the chosen features for the individual machine learning approach, but we have also seen that the differences along the languages are very subtle. Most approaches do not show a clear preference for one specific language. Also, the differences are difficult to interpret because the results of the baseline classifiers for each language are very far apart from each other and the variety caused by different classifiers is much bigger than the language dependency.

The evaluated approaches performed better on English texts than on German. Whenever an approach improved according to the English baseline, this approach also improved according to the German baseline.

Focusing on the chosen features, we have seen that using large numbers of unigrams is more useful for English, compared to using only POS-tags. Since there is no objective comparison value, it remains unclear if this means that POS-tags are less useful or unigrams more useful for English. We have furthermore observed that POS-trigrams are more useful for German. These two aspects indicate that German subjectivity is more grammaticalized as opposed to English subjectivity which is more based in lexis.

Another feature that seems to be more useful for German are the long-distance-bigrams.

The efficacy of the minimum-cut approach strongly depends on the distribution of class labels in the articles. If many sentences are tagged with the same labels as their neighbors, the approach will be very useful, otherwise it will not. In the evaluation we found that the approach seems to work slightly better for MPQA than for SGN. The statistics about the corpora confirm this, indicating that MPQA has more consecutive sentences with equal annotations (see Table 1).

Another important observation we made is that machine-translation of training data is not a viable alternative to manually creating it. The results only came close to their comparison values for approaches that did not perform so well in the first place. The effectiveness of the approach depends of course on the quality of the translation. So it can be expected that it becomes more useful in the future as machine-translation improves. On the other hand, the quality of translations between English and German is quite high compared to other language pairs.

Summarizing we can state that there is no subjectivity detection approach which is more suitable for German texts than for English texts.

The dataset was published at `http://130.149.154.91/corpus/snc/SNC.de.zip`.

References

Carmen Banea, Rada Mihalcea, Janyce Wiebe, and Samer Hassan. 2008. Multilingual subjectivity analysis using machine translation. In *Proceedings of the EMNLP '08*, pages 127–135, Morristown, NJ, USA. Association for Computational Linguistics.

Ann Banfield. 1982. *Unspeakable sentence*. Routledge.

Bo Chen, Hui He, and Jun Guo. 2007. Language feature mining for document subjectivity analysis. In *ISDPE '07: First International Symposium on Data, Privacy, and E-Commerce*, pages 62–67, Washington, DC, USA. IEEE Computer Society.

Amitava Das and Sivaji Bandyopadhyay. 2009. Subjectivity detection in english and bengali: A crf-based approach. In *Proceedings of ICON 2009*, Hyderabad.

Bo Pang and Lillian Lee. 2004. A sentimental education: Sentiment analysis using subjectivity summarization based on minimum cuts. In *Proc. of the ACL*, pages 271–278.

Bo Pang, Lillian Lee, and Shivakumar Vaithyanathan. 2002. Thumbs up? Sentiment classification using machine learning techniques. In *Proceedings of the EMNLP '02*, pages 79–86.

Randolph Quirk. 1985. *A comprehensive grammar of the English language*. Longman.

Ellen Riloff, Janyce Wiebe, and Theresa Wilson. 2003. Learning subjective nouns using extraction pattern bootstrapping. In *Proceedings of the seventh conference on Natural language learning at HLT-NAACL 2003*, pages 25–32, Morristown, NJ, USA. Association for Computational Linguistics.

M. Santini. 2004. A shallow approach to syntactic feature extraction for genre classification. In *Proceedings of the 7th Annual Colloquium for the UK Special Interest Group for Computational Linguistics*.

Janyce Wiebe, Theresa Wilson, Rebecca Bruce, Matthew Bell, and Melanie Martin. 2004. Learning subjective language. *Computational Linguistics*, 30(3):277– 308, January.

Janyce Wiebe. 2002. Instructions for annotating opinions in newspaper articles. Technical report, University of Pittsburgh.

Hui Yang, Luo Si, and Jamie Callan. 2006. Knowledge transfer and opinion detection in the TREC2006 blog track. In *Proceedings of TREC*.

Hong Yu and Vasileios Hatzivassiloglou. 2003. Separating facts from opinions and identifying the polarity of opinion sentences. In *Proc. of EMNLP '03*, pages 129–136.

Learning to Extract Protein–Protein Interactions using Distant Supervision

Philippe Thomas [1] **Illés Solt** [1,2] **Roman Klinger** [3] **Ulf Leser** [1]

[1]Knowledge Management in Bioinformatics, Institute for Computer Science, Humboldt-Universität zu Berlin, Unter den Linden 6, 10099 Berlin, Germany
{thomas, leser}@informatik.hu-berlin.de

[2]Dept. of Telecommunications and Media Informatics, Budapest University of Technology, Magyar tudósok körútja 2, 1117 Budapest, Hungary
solt@tmit.bme.hu

[3]Fraunhofer Institute for Algorithms and Scientific Computing SCAI, Fraunhofer-Gesellschaft, Schloss Birlinghoven, 53754 Sankt Augustin, Germany
roman.klinger@scai.fraunhofer.de

Abstract

Most relation extraction methods, especially in the domain of biology, rely on machine learning methods to classify a co-occurring pair of entities in a sentence to be related or not. Such an approach requires a training corpus, which involves expert annotation and is tedious, time-consuming, and expensive.

We overcome this problem by the use of existing knowledge in structured databases to automatically generate a training corpus for protein-protein interactions. An extensive evaluation of different instance selection strategies is performed to maximize robustness on this presumably noisy resource. Successful strategies to consistently improve performance include a majority voting ensemble of classifiers trained on subsets of the training corpus and the use of knowledge bases consisting of proven non-interactions. Our best configured model built without manually annotated data shows very competitive results on several publicly available benchmark corpora.

1 Introduction

Protein function depends, to a large degree, on the functional context of its interaction partners, *e.g.* other proteins or metabolites. Accordingly, getting a better understanding of protein-protein interactions (PPIs) is vital to understand biological processes within organisms. Several databases, such as IntAct, DIP, or MINT, contain detailed information about these interactions. To populate such databases, curators extract experimentally validated PPIs from peer reviewed publications (Ceol et al., 2010). Therefore, the automated extraction of PPIs from publications for assisting database curators has attracted considerable attention (Hakenberg et al., 2008; Airola et al., 2008; Tikk et al., 2010; Bui et al., 2010).

PPI extraction is usually tackled by classifying the $\binom{n}{2}$ undirected protein mention pairs within a sentence, where n is the number of protein mentions in the sentence. Classification of such pairs is often approached by machine learning (Airola et al., 2008; Tikk et al., 2010) or pattern-based methods (Fundel et al., 2007; Hakenberg et al., 2008) both requiring manually annotated corpora, which are costly to obtain and often biased to the annotation guidelines and corpus selection criteria. To overcome this issue, recent work has concentrated on distant supervision and multiple instance learning (Bunescu and Mooney, 2007; Mintz et al., 2009). Instead of manually annotated corpora, such approaches infer training instances from non-annotated texts using knowledge bases, thus allowing to increase the training set size by a few orders of magnitude. Corpora derived by distant supervision are inherently noisy, thus benefiting from robust classification methods.

1.1 Previous work

Distant supervision for relation extraction has recently gained considerable attention. Approaches usually focus on non-biomedical relations, such as "author wrote book" (Brin, 1999) or "person born in city" (Bunescu and Mooney, 2007). This work highlighted that it is feasible to train a classifier using distant supervision, which culminated in ideas to learn literally thousands of classifiers from relational databases like Freebase (Mintz et al., 2009; Yao et al., 2010), Yago (Nguyen and Moschitti, 2011), or Wikipedia infoboxes (Hoffmann et al., 2010).

So far, approaches in the biomedical domain on distant supervision focused on pattern learning (Hakenberg et al., 2008; Abacha and Zweigenbaum, 2010; Thomas et al., 2011). This is surprising as statistical machine learning methods are most commonly used for relation extraction. For example, only one of the five best performing systems in the BioNLP 2011 shared task relied on patterns (Kim et al., 2011).

The approaches described by Hakenberg et al. (2008) and Thomas et al. (2011) are those most related to our work. Both approaches learn a set of initial patterns by extracting sentences from MEDLINE potentially describing protein-protein interactions. Both methods use a knowledge base (IntAct) as input and search sentences containing protein pairs known to interact according to the knowledge base. However, these approaches generate patterns only for positive training instances and ignore the information contained in the remaining presumably negative instances.

PPI extraction is one of the most extensively studied relation extraction problems in the biomedical domain and is perfectly suited for a study on distant supervision as several corpora have been published in a common format (Pyysalo et al., 2008). Pyysalo et al. showed that the corpora differ in many aspects, *e.g.* annotation guidelines, average sentence length, and most importantly in the ratio of positive to negative training instances which accounts for about 50 % of all performance differences. Related work by Airola et al. (2008) and Tikk et al. (2010) revealed that the relation extraction performance substantially decreases when the evaluation corpus has different properties than the training corpus. A basic overview of the five most commonly used benchmark PPI corpora is given in Table 1.

So far, it is unclear how distant supervision performs on the difficult tasks of PPI extraction. For example Nguyen and Moschitti (2011) achieve a F_1 of 74.3 % on 52 different Yago relations using distant supervision. On the other hand, completely supervised state-of-the-art PPI extraction using manually labeled corpora achieve F_1 ranging from 56.5 % (AIMed) to 76.8 % (LLL) depending on the complexity of the corpus (Airola et al., 2008).

Corpus	Pairs		Class ratio
	positive	negative	$\frac{\text{positive}}{\text{negative}}$
AIMed	1,000	4,834	0.21
BioInfer	2,534	7,132	0.35
HPRD50	163	270	0.60
IEPA	335	482	0.73
LLL	164	166	0.99

Table 1: Overview of the 5 corpora used for evaluation. For state-of-the-art results on these corpora, see Table 3.

The contribution of the work described herein is as follows: We present different variations of strategies to utilize distant supervision for PPI extraction in Section 2. The potential benefit for PPI extraction is evaluated. Parameters taken into account are the number of training instances as well as the ratio of positive to negative examples. Finally, we assess if an ensemble of classifiers can further improve classification performance.

2 Methods

In this section, the workflow to extract interaction pairs from the databases and to generate training instances is described. Additionally, the configuration of the classifier applied to this corpus is given followed by the outline of the experimental setting.

2.1 Generation of training data

Training instances are generated as follows. All MEDLINE abstracts published between 1985 and 2011 are split into sentences using the sentence segmentation model by Buyko et al. (2006) and scanned for gene and protein names using GNAT (Hakenberg et al., 2011). In total, we find 1,312,059 sentences with 8,324,763 protein pairs. To avoid information leakage between training and test sets, articles contained in any of the benchmark evaluation corpora have been removed. This procedure excludes 7,476 ($< 0.1\%$) protein mention pairs from the training set. Protein pairs that are contained in the PPI knowledge base IntAct[1] (Aranda et al., 2010) are labeled as positive instances. Following a *closed world assumption*, protein pairs not contained in IntAct are considered as negative instances.

[1] As of Mar 24, 2010.

It is very likely, that both negative and positive instances contain a certain amount of mislabeled examples (false positives, false negatives). Therefore, we utilize different heuristics to minimize the amount of mislabeled instances. Firstly, we generate a list of words, which are frequently employed to indicate an interaction between two proteins [2]. This list is used to filter positive and negative instances such that positive instances contain at least one interaction word (*pos-iword*) and negative contain no interaction word (*neg-iword*). Application of both filters in combination is referred to as *pos/neg-iword*. Secondly, we assume that sentences with only two proteins are more likely to describe a relationship between these two proteins than sentences which contain many protein names. This filter is called *pos-pair*. For the sake of completeness, it is tested on negative instances alone (*neg-pair*) and on positive and negative instances in combination (*pos/neg-pair*). All seven experiments are summarized in Table 2.

2.2 Classification and experimental settings

For classification, we use a support vector machine with the shallow linguistic (SL) kernel (Giuliano et al., 2006) which has been previously shown to generate state-of-the-art results for PPI extraction (Tikk et al., 2010). This method uses syntactic features, *e.g.* word, stem, part-of-speech tag and morphologic properties of the surrounding words to train a classifier, but no parse tree information.

Setting	Feature:	Interaction word count		Pairs in sentence	
	Condition:	≥ 1	$= 0$	$= 1$	$= 1$
	Applied to:	positive	negative	positive	negative
baseline					
pos-iword		•			
neg-iword			•		
pos/neg-iword		•	•		
pos-pair				•	
neg-pair					•
pos/neg-pair				•	•

Table 2: Our experiment settings. Based on the number of interaction words and protein mention pairs in the containing sentence, we filter out automatically generated positive or negative example pairs not meeting the indicated heuristic condition. The dots indicate which filter is applied for which setting. For instance no filtering takes place for the baseline setting.

[2]`http://www2.informatik.hu-berlin.de/~thomas/pub/iwords.txt`

Classifiers are trained with a small subset from all 8 Million pairs, using 50,000 instances in all experiments except when stated differently. This allows us to investigate systematic differences between settings instead of generating and comparing only one prediction per setting.

Classifiers often tend to keep the same positive to negative ratio seen during the training phase. Class imbalance is therefore often acknowledged as a serious problem (Chawla et al., 2004). In our first experiments, we set the positive to negative ratio according to the overall ratio of positive to negative instances of all five corpora excluding the test corpus. This allows us to compare the results with the performance of various state-of-the-art kernel methods. As few publications provide results for the so-called cross-learning scenario, where a classifier is trained on the ensemble of four corpora and tested on the fifth corpus, we take the results from the extensive benchmark conducted by Tikk et al. (2010).

The influence of training class imbalance is evaluated separately by varying training set positive to negative ratios from 0.001 to $1,000$ using the best filtering strategy from the previous experiment.

As a sentence may describe a true protein interaction not present in the knowledge base, the closed world assumption is likely to be violated. Furthermore, not all mentions of a pair of proteins known to interact will describe an interaction. Thus both positively and negatively inferred training instances can be considered noisy. We therefore experimented with another filtering technique by using the Negatome database[3] (Smialowski et al., 2010) as an additional source to infer negative examples. Negatome contains a reference set of *non-interacting* protein pairs and is thus better suited to infer negative examples than our current method, which infers a negative example for all protein pairs not contained in the knowledge base according to the closed world assumption. However, reliable information about non-interaction is substantially more difficult to obtain and therefore the database contains far less entries than IntAct. From our 8 million protein pairs only 6,005 pairs could be labeled as negative. Additional negative training instances required for the training phase are therefore inferred using the closed world assumption.

[3]As of April 30, 2011.

Further, we evaluate how much training data is required to successfully train a classifier and if the classifier reaches a steady state after a certain number of training instances.

Finally, we evaluate whether a majority voting ensemble of 11 classifiers trained on randomly drawn training instances can further improve extraction quality. This strategy loosely follows a bagging strategy (Breiman, 1996), however, training instances are suspected to be less overlapping than using the standard bagging strategy.

2.3 Evaluation

For evaluation, we use the five benchmark PPI corpora listed in Table 1. Each training procedure, except for the ensemble experiments, is repeated 10 times randomly, thus resulting in 10 independent estimates for precision, recall, F_1, and area under the ROC curve (AUC). This allows for robust estimation of all evaluation metrics. Using single sided MannWhitney U test (Mann and Whitney, 1947) p-values for F_1 and AUC between two different models are calculated, with the null hypothesis that median of two samples is equal. Significance of Kendall correlation is determined using Best and Gipps (1974) with the null hypothesis that correlation equals zero. For all tests we assume a p-value of 0.01 to determine significance.

3 Results

Mean values for the seven different instance selection strategies (introduced in Table 2) are shown in Table 3. All strategies, except *neg-pair* filtering, lead to a higher AUC than 0.5. Thus six of seven settings perform better than randomly guessing. The advantage over random guessing is generally significant, except for three experiments in LLL. Many instance selection strategies for AIMed, BioInfer and HPRD50 outperform co-occurrence in terms of F_1. Several experiments outperform or at least perform on a par with the results from Thomas et al. (2011).

Co-occurrence outperforms significantly all seven settings for the two remaining corpora IEPA and LLL in F_1. This might have several reasons: First, these two corpora have the highest fraction of positive instances, therefore co-occurrence is a very strong baseline. Second, IEPA describes chemical relations instead of PPIs, thus our training instances might not properly reflect the syntactic property of such relations.

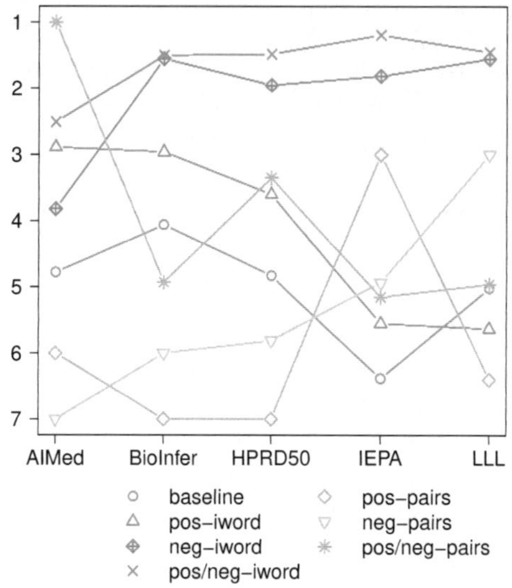

Figure 1: Average rank in F_1 for each experiment setting on the five corpora.

It is encouraging that on two corpora (BioInfer and HPRD50) the best setting performs about on par with the best cross-learning results from Tikk et al., which have been generated using manually annotated data and are therefore suspected to produce superior results.

For each corpus, we calculate and visualize the average rank in F_1 for the seven different strategies (see Figure 1). This figure indicates that pos/neg-iword and neg-iword filtering perform very well.

Repeating the previously described instance selection strategies (see Table 2) using Negatome to infer negative training instances lead to a small increase of 0.5 percentage points (pp) in F_1, due to an average increase of 1.1 pp in precision over all five corpora and seven settings (Results shown at bottom of Table 3). We also observe a tendency for increased AUC (0.9 pp). The largest gain in precision (3.5 pp) is observed between the two baseline results where no instance filtering is applied. Results for varied positive to negative ratios and for various amounts of training instances are also contained in the same table and visualized in Figure 2a and 2b respectively.

4 Discussion

The various settings introduced to filter out likely noisy training instances either improved precision or recall or both over the baseline using all automatically labeled instances for training (data shown in Table 3). In the following, we analyze and compare these settings.

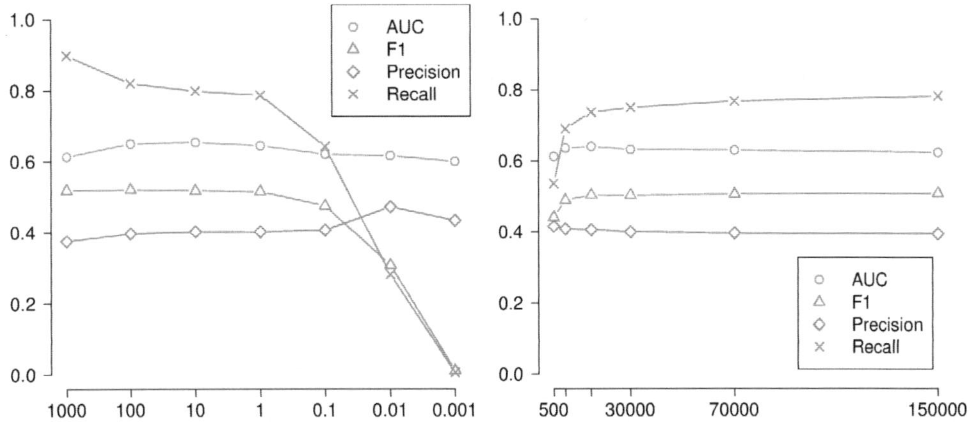

(a) Positive to negative ratio (b) Sample size

Figure 2: Distribution of mean precision, recall, F_1, and AUC depending for the evaluation of class imbalance and sample size.

Method		AIMed				BioInfer				HPRD50				IEPA				LLL			
		AUC	P	R	F_1	AUC	P	R	F_1	AUC	P	R	F_1	AUC	P	R	F_1	AUC	P	R	F_1
co-occurrence			17.8	(100)	30.1		26.6	(100)	41.7		38.9	(100)	55.4		40.8	(100)	57.6		55.9	(100)	70.3
supervised (Tikk et al.)		77.5	28.3	86.6	42.6	74.9	62.8	36.5	46.2	78.0	56.9	68.7	62.2	75.6	71.0	52.5	60.4	79.5	79.0	57.3	66.4
semi-supervised (Thomas et al.)			25.8	62.9	36.6		43.4	50.3	46.6		48.3	51.5	49.9		67.5	58.2	62.5		70.3	70.7	70.5
Setting	baseline	65.1	21.0	82.8	33.5	63.2	33.3	64.2	43.8	64.4	42.8	75.4	54.6	52.2	40.9	11.6	18.0	51.8	51.3	39.2	44.4
	pos-iword	66.6	21.8	82.6	34.5	67.5	38.4	60.8	47.1	67.5	45.5	76.5	57.1	53.8	48.6	12.3	19.6	51.6	50.0	37.0	42.2
	neg-iword	65.3	21.1	**91.1**	34.2	68.1	37.3	70.9	48.9	**73.4**	43.9	**93.6**	59.8	54.7	43.9	49.9	46.7	53.9	49.9	**77.4**	60.7
	pos/neg-iword	65.1	21.4	89.8	34.6	68.6	38.6	67.0	**49.0**	73.3	44.8	93.2	**60.5**	54.6	43.8	**53.2**	**48.0**	53.5	50.7	75.8	**60.8**
	pos-pairs	64.2	**29.3**	33.4	31.2	**69.8**	**57.8**	18.0	27.5	62.7	**47.9**	35.6	40.8	**66.6**	**54.9**	26.3	35.5	**63.2**	**68.2**	27.8	39.5
	neg-pairs	46.9	17.2	85.5	28.6	37.3	24.4	**85.6**	37.9	50.8	39.0	80.9	52.6	36.5	22.4	18.6	20.3	38.2	44.7	66.2	53.3
	pos/neg-pairs	**69.7**	23.6	82.3	**36.6**	62.0	32.8	60.6	42.5	69.2	46.5	75.2	57.5	56.0	43.4	13.3	20.3	54.3	54.5	37.9	44.6
Train pos/neg ratio	1,000	60.6	19.0	89.8	31.3	64.2	31.3	**84.6**	45.7	62.5	41.1	92.9	57.0	57.9	42.6	**88.3**	**57.3**	61.2	53.7	**93.3**	**68.1**
	100	63.9	20.0	88.7	32.7	69.0	35.5	77.8	48.7	71.5	44.2	91.9	59.6	**58.9**	45.6	65.6	53.7	**61.5**	53.1	85.8	65.6
	10	65.5	20.9	91.0	33.9	**71.2**	38.7	76.0	**51.2**	74.1	44.2	**95.8**	60.5	57.9	45.7	55.5	50.1	57.9	51.8	80.7	63.1
	1	65.6	21.4	**91.1**	34.7	70.0	38.6	71.3	50.1	**74.5**	44.3	95.5	**60.6**	56.1	45.0	55.5	49.7	55.7	51.6	79.3	62.5
	0.1	65.4	22.3	81.3	**35.0**	67.9	40.9	57.9	48.0	72.1	46.9	84.7	60.4	53.5	43.1	37.9	40.3	51.0	50.0	58.7	53.9
	0.01	**66.0**	26.9	46.7	34.1	66.5	46.9	24.7	32.4	70.4	59.7	48.5	53.4	52.8	**48.2**	8.3	14.2	52.2	**54.3**	12.3	19.7
	0.001	61.5	**41.4**	0.9	1.8	63.2	**63.0**	0.3	0.6	67.8	**72.5**	1.3	2.6	53.0	30.0	0.1	0.2	54.1	10.0	0.1	0.1
Train set size	500	63.4	**21.8**	71.5	33.4	65.9	39.8	44.6	41.9	67.6	**48.4**	67.4	56.2	55.5	45.4	31.5	36.7	54.0	**52.6**	53.4	52.7
	5,000	65.3	21.4	84.3	34.2	69.0	**39.9**	63.5	48.9	72.6	45.7	89.0	60.4	**56.8**	**46.1**	**41.9**	43.8	54.5	51.3	66.3	57.8
	15,000	**65.5**	**21.6**	87.9	**34.6**	**69.1**	39.7	65.1	**49.3**	**74.2**	45.6	92.9	**61.2**	55.8	44.5	47.4	45.9	**55.7**	51.9	75.1	61.3
	30,000	65.3	21.5	89.4	**34.6**	68.8	39.2	66.5	**49.3**	73.0	44.6	**93.1**	60.3	55.0	44.0	50.7	47.1	53.8	50.9	75.2	60.7
	70,000	65.1	21.3	90.7	**34.6**	68.6	38.1	67.4	48.7	73.2	44.2	92.1	59.8	54.2	43.7	55.0	48.7	53.9	50.9	78.6	61.8
	150,000	64.7	21.3	**91.3**	34.5	68.2	37.5	**68.1**	48.4	73.1	44.1	92.8	59.8	53.0	43.0	57.1	**49.1**	52.7	51.1	**81.3**	**62.7**
Setting (+Negatome)	baseline	65.9	22.2	79.6	34.7	65.7	36.8	58.6	45.2	67.6	46.7	74.0	57.3	54.9	47.5	12.7	20.0	54.8	53.6	36.3	43.2
	pos-iword	67.4	22.9	81.4	35.8	69.1	41.1	56.3	47.5	69.2	**47.9**	75.4	58.5	57.4	52.6	12.9	20.6	52.3	51.2	37.5	43.1
	neg-iword	65.3	21.1	**90.7**	34.3	68.8	38.1	69.6	**49.2**	**73.6**	44.6	92.1	60.1	55.6	44.4	51.7	47.8	55.2	51.3	**78.9**	62.2
	pos/neg-iword	65.1	21.4	89.4	34.6	68.8	38.8	66.9	49.1	73.2	44.8	**92.2**	**60.3**	55.3	44.2	**53.8**	**48.5**	54.9	52.2	77.9	**62.5**
	pos-pairs	64.6	**29.6**	33.7	31.5	**69.7**	**58.2**	18.3	27.8	62.2	48.5	35.5	41.0	**66.9**	**56.6**	30.7	39.7	**63.4**	**68.8**	28.1	39.9
	neg-pairs	47.0	17.2	84.9	28.6	37.0	24.3	**85.0**	37.8	50.9	38.4	79.8	51.9	36.0	22.4	18.5	20.3	38.5	45.1	66.0	53.5
	pos/neg-pairs	**69.8**	23.8	81.1	**36.8**	63.9	34.6	58.6	43.5	69.5	47.5	74.2	57.9	57.0	44.3	13.9	21.1	54.7	53.2	34.5	41.7

Table 3: Results of different instance selection strategies, different positive to negative ratios in the training set, sample size and employing Negatome as negative knowledge base.

Method	AIMed				BioInfer				HPRD50				IEPA				LLL			
	AUC	P	R	F_1	AUC	P	R	F_1	AUC	P	R	F_1	AUC	P	R	F_1	AUC	P	R	F_1
co-occurrence		17.8	(100)	30.1		26.6	(100)	41.7		38.9	(100)	55.4		40.8	(100)	57.6		55.9	(100)	70.3
supervised (Tikk et. al)	77.5	28.3	86.6	42.6	74.9	62.8	36.5	46.2	78.0	56.9	68.7	62.2	75.6	71.0	52.5	60.4	79.5	79.0	57.3	66.4
semi-supervised (Thomas et. al)		25.8	62.9	36.6		43.4	50.3	46.6		48.3	51.5	49.9		67.5	58.2	62.5		70.3	70.7	70.5
mean of 11 runs	65.5	21.4	90.9	34.6	69.9	70.7	38.9	50.2	74.0	44.4	94.7	60.4	55.5	44.7	54.6	49.1	55.2	50.6	78.0	61.4
bagging over 11 runs		21.4	91.3	34.7		70.9	39.3	50.6		44.3	95.1	60.4		44.4	53.1	48.3		49.8	77.4	60.6

Table 4: Result of bagging over 11 classifier trained on different subsets. For comparison we show the average results for these 11 runs.

4.1 Pair count based settings

From our analysis it becomes apparent that no correlation between AUC and F_1 exists (Kendall's tau = 0.23, p-value = 0.55). For example pos-pair filtering significantly outperforms on three corpora all remaining six settings in terms of AUC, but the same setting supersedes almost no other setting in terms of F_1. A closer look reveals that on all five corpora the highest average precision can be achieved with this setting, at the cost of a decrease in recall. The pos-pair selection strategy results in fairly good training instances, but the decision hyperplane is not appropriately set.

The opposing filtering strategy (neg-pair) outperforms no other method in terms of AUC with an average score often below or at least close to a random classifier. However, this is expected, as the classifier tends to assign negative class labels to all sentences with exactly two protein mentions. This filter is in direct conflict to the original motivation and demonstrates that filtering must be performed carefully.

Even though positive and negative training instance filtering alone lead to almost no increase in F_1, the filtering of both negative and positive pairs leads to an overall improvement of 1.44 pp.

4.2 Interaction word based settings

All different combinations of instance filtering using a list of interaction words lead to an overall increase in F_1 and AUC. Filtering of positive and negative instances (pos/neg-iword) leads to the highest increase in AUC and with 11.8 pp in F_1, followed with 11.3 pp by exclusively filtering negative instances (neg-iword). Finally we observe only a marginal improvement of 1.3 pp when filtering positive instances (pos-iword).

4.3 Experiments with Negatome

A clear drawback of Negatome is the comparable small sample size of protein pairs. The number of confidently negative training instances could be increased by generalizing proteins across species using, for instance, Homologene. On our data set we could infer approximately 4,200 additional training instances. However, it is unclear if these derived instances are of the same quality than the Negatome data set. Another possibility is the usage of additional text repositories.

4.4 Effect of the pos/neg ratio

Table 3 clearly indicates that positive to negative ratio on training data affects performance of a classifier. Precision and recall strongly correlate with the pos/neg ratio seen in the training set. The observed correlation between recall and pos/neg ratio (Kendall's tau ranging from 0.524 to 1 for all five corpora) is expected, as the classifier tends to assign more test instances to the majority (positive) class. This procedure works best for corpora with many positive examples. A strong correlation (Kendall's tau ranging from -0.9 to -1.0) between precision and class ratio can be observed for AIMed, BioInfer, and HPRD50. Correlation for IEPA is close to zero and for LLL the correlation is even positive but not significant (p-value of 0.13). Overall, the observed influence is less pronounced than expected. For instance F_1 remains comparably robust with an average standard deviation of 2.6 pp for ratios between 0.1 and 10 . With more pronounced differences in the training ratio, a strong impact on F_1 can be observed.

In contrast to previous work on distant supervision, more noise on positive and negative instances is expected as database knowledge is suspected to be less complete and besides incompleteness knowledge evolves faster than for example for "president of country" relations. Other approaches often deal only with a strong noise on positive data, but little noise on negative instances. To avoid the double sided noise, we experimented with one class variations of SVM (Schölkopf et al., 2001) exploring the identical feature space. In one class classification only instances for the target set are available and the classifier searches a separating boundary between instances and yet unseen outliers. It has been previously demonstrated that one class classifiers are less sensitive to highly imbalanced data (Raskutti and Kowalczyk, 2004; Dreiseitl et al., 2010). However, in our experiments one class classifiers constantly achieved results close to random classification regardless of whether we used solely positive or negative instances for training.

4.5 Effect of training set size

For all corpora except for HPRD50 a monotonic increase in recall (Kendall's Tau of 1; p-value < 0.01) can be observed while increasing the training set. The negative correlation between precision and sample size is less pronounced but still observable for all Corpora (Kendall's Tau ranges between -0.552 and -1). Subsequently F_1 increases for corpora with many positive instances. Presumably, the problem of class imbalance gets more pronounced with additional instances.

4.6 Bagging

On the settings previously identified of being superior, we trained 11 classifiers using randomly sampled training sets. That is, a filtering of positive and negative instances for interaction words, a positive to negative ratio of 1, and a training size of 15,000 instances. The average results of the trained classifiers and the result of majority voting are given in Table 4. The ensemble classifier performs about on par with the mean of the individual classifiers and we observe no significant difference between the two approaches. However, a single classifier sometimes performs better or worse than the ensemble, whereas bagging always performs close to the mean result. Thus, bagging can be successfully applied for improving robustness of a classifier. Note that in our setting, all votes are of equal importance, thus neglecting the fact that some classifier perform generally better than others.

5 Conclusion

We investigated the use of distant supervision and demonstrated that it can be successfully adopted for domains where named entity recognition and normalization is still an unsolved issue and the closed world assumption might be an unsupported stretch. This is important, as named entity recognition and normalization is a key requirement for distant supervision. Distant supervision is therefore an extremely valuable method and allows training classifiers for virtually all kinds of relationships for which a database exists. We have proven here that results obtained without a manually annotated corpus are competitive with purely supervised methods, thus the tedious task of annotating a training corpus can be avoided.

Using five benchmark evaluation corpora – having diverse properties, annotated by different researchers adhering to differing annotation guidelines – offers a perfect opportunity to evaluate the robustness and usability of distant supervision. Our analysis reveals that background knowledge such as interaction words or "negative" knowledge bases such as Negatome consistently improves results across all five corpora. Also bagging had a positive impact on classifier robustness.

Surprisingly, class imbalance seams to be a less pronounced problem in distant supervision as often observed for supervised settings. One possible explanation might be that due to the noisy data, a classifier is less prone to over-fitting. So far, our experiments with one-class classification algorithms trained on positive or negative examples solely lead to disappointing results with AUC scores close to that of a random classifier. In future work, we plan to investigate if other one-class algorithms can be successfully adapted for relation extraction in a distant supervised setting.

Instance selection seems to have the largest impact for this approach. Instead of simple heuristics, we plan to investigate the usability of syntactic patterns to further discriminate positive and negative instances (Bui et al., 2010).

References

A.B. Abacha and P. Zweigenbaum. 2010. Automatic Extraction of semantic relations between medical entities: Application to the treatment relation. In *Proc. of SMBM 2010.*

A. Airola, S. Pyysalo, J. Björne, T. Pahikkala, F. Ginter, and T. Salakoski. 2008. All-paths graph kernel for protein-protein interaction extraction with evaluation of cross-corpus learning. *BMC Bioinformatics*, 9 Suppl 11:S2.

B. Aranda, P. Achuthan, Y. Alam-Faruque, I. Armean, A. Bridge, C. Derow, M. Feuermann, A. T. Ghanbarian, S. Kerrien, J. Khadake, J. Kerssemakers, C. Leroy, M. Menden, M. Michaut, L. Montecchi-Palazzi, S. N. Neuhauser, S. Orchard, V. Perreau, B. Roechert, K. van Eijk, and H. Hermjakob. 2010. The IntAct molecular interaction database in 2010. *Nucleic Acids Res*, 38:525–531, Jan.

D. J. Best and P. G. Gipps. 1974. Algorithm AS 71: The Upper Tail Probabilities of Kendall's Tau. *Journal of the Royal Statistical Society.*, 23(1):pp. 98–100.

L. Breiman. 1996. Bagging Predictors. *Machine Learning*, 24(2):123–140.

S. Brin. 1999. Extracting Patterns and Relations from the World Wide Web. Technical Report 1999-65, Stanford InfoLab, November.

Q. Bui, S. Katrenko, and P. M. A. Sloot. 2010. A hybrid approach to extract protein-protein interactions. *Bioinformatics*, Nov.

R. C. Bunescu and R. J. Mooney. 2007. Learning to Extract Relations from the Web using Minimal Supervision. In *Proc. of ACL'07.*

E. Buyko, J. Wermter, M. Poprat, and U. Hahn. 2006. Automatically Adapting an NLP Core Engine to the Biology Domain. In *Proc. of ISMB'2006.*

A. Ceol, A. Chatr-aryamontri, L. Licata, D. Peluso, L. Briganti, L. Perfetto, L. Castagnoli, and G. Cesareni. 2010. MINT, the molecular interaction database: 2009 update. *Nucl. Acids Res.*, 38(suppl1):D532–539.

N.V. Chawla, N. Japkowicz, and A. Kotcz. 2004. Editorial: special issue on learning from imbalanced data sets. *ACM SIGKDD Explorations Newsletter*, 6(1):1–6.

S. Dreiseitl, M. Osl, C. Scheibböck, and M. Binder. 2010. Outlier Detection with One-Class SVMs: An Application to Melanoma Prognosis. *AMIA Annu Symp Proc*, 2010:172–176.

K. Fundel, R. Küffner, and R. Zimmer. 2007. RelEx–relation extraction using dependency parse trees. *Bioinformatics*, 23(3):365–371, Feb.

C. Giuliano, A. Lavelli, and L. Romano. 2006. Exploiting Shallow Linguistic Information for Relation Extraction from Biomedical Literature. In *Proc. of EACL'06.*

J. Hakenberg, C. Plake, L.Royer, H. Strobelt, U. Leser, and M. Schroeder. 2008. Gene mention normalization and interaction extraction with context models and sentence motifs. *Genome Biol*, 9 Suppl 2:S14.

J. Hakenberg, M. Gerner, M. Haeussler, I. Solt, C. Plake, M. Schroeder, G. Gonzalez, G. Nenadic, and C.M. Bergman. 2011. The GNAT library for local and remote gene mention normalization. *Bioinformatics*, Aug.

R. Hoffmann, C. Zhang, and D. Weld. 2010. Learning 5000 relational extractors. In *Proc. of ACL'10*, pages 286–295.

J. Kim, Y. Wang, T. Takagi, and A. Yonezawa. 2011. Overview of genia event task in bionlp shared task 2011. In *Proc. of BioNLP-ST 2011*, pages 7–15.

H. B. Mann and D. R. Whitney. 1947. On a test of whether one of two random variables is stochastically larger than the other. *Annals of Mathematical Statistics.*

M. Mintz, S. Bills, R. Snow, and D. Jurafsky. 2009. Distant supervision for relation extraction without labeled data. In *Proc. of AFNLP*, volume 2 of *ACL '09*, pages 1003–1011.

T.V. Nguyen and A. Moschitti. 2011. End-to-End Relation Extraction Using Distant Supervision from External Semantic Repositories. In *ACL'2011*, pages 277–282.

S. Pyysalo, A. Airola, J. Heimonen, J. Björne, F. Ginter, and T. Salakoski. 2008. Comparative analysis of five protein-protein interaction corpora. *BMC Bioinformatics*, 9 Suppl 3:S6.

B. Raskutti and A. Kowalczyk. 2004. Extreme rebalancing for SVMs: a case study. *ACM SIGKDD Explorations Newsletter*, 6(1):60–69.

B. Schölkopf, J. C. Platt, J. Shawe-Taylor, A. J. Smola, and R. C. Williamson. 2001. Estimating the support of a high-dimensional distribution. *Neural Comput*, 13(7):1443–1471, Jul.

P. Smialowski, P. Pagel, P. Wong, B. Brauner, I. Dunger, G. Fobo, G. Frishman, C. Montrone, T. Rattei, D. Frishman, and A. Ruepp. 2010. The Negatome database: a reference set of non-interacting protein pairs. *Nucleic Acids Res*, 38:D540–D544, Jan.

P. Thomas, S. Pietschmann, I. Solt, D. Tikk, and U. Leser. 2011. Not all links are equal: Exploiting dependency types for the extraction of protein-protein interactions from text. In *Proc. of BioNLP'11.*

D. Tikk, P. Thomas, P. Palaga, J. Hakenberg, and U. Leser. 2010. A comprehensive benchmark of kernel methods to extract protein-protein interactions from literature. *PLoS Comput Biol*, 6.

L. Yao, S. Riedel, and A. McCallum. 2010. Collective cross-document relation extraction without labelled data. In *Proc. of EMNLP'10*, pages 1013–1023.

Topic Models with Logical Constraints on Words

Hayato Kobayashi **Hiromi Wakaki** **Tomohiro Yamasaki** **Masaru Suzuki**
Research and Development Center,
Toshiba Corporation, Japan
{hayato.kobayashi, hiromi.wakaki,
tomohiro2.yamasaki, masaru1.suzuki}@toshiba.co.jp

Abstract

This paper describes a simple method to achieve logical constraints on words for topic models based on a recently developed topic modeling framework with Dirichlet forest priors (LDA-DF). Logical constraints mean logical expressions of pairwise constraints, *Must-links* and *Cannot-Links*, used in the literature of constrained clustering. Our method can not only cover the original constraints of the existing work, but also allow us easily to add new customized constraints. We discuss the validity of our method by defining its asymptotic behaviors. We verify the effectiveness of our method with comparative studies on a synthetic corpus and interactive topic analysis on a real corpus.

1 Introduction

Topic models such as Latent Dirichlet Allocation or LDA (Blei et al., 2003) are widely used to capture hidden topics in a corpus. When we have domain knowledge of a target corpus, incorporating the knowledge into topic models would be useful in a practical sense. Thus there have been many studies of semi-supervised extensions of topic models (Andrzejewski et al., 2007; Toutanova and Johnson, 2008; Andrzejewski et al., 2009; Andrzejewski and Zhu, 2009), although topic models are often regarded as unsupervised learning. Recently, (Andrzejewski et al., 2009) developed a novel topic modeling framework, LDA with Dirichlet Forest priors (LDA-DF), which achieves two links *Must-Link* (*ML*) and *Cannot-Link* (*CL*) in the constrained clustering literature (Basu et al., 2008). For given words A and B, $ML(A, B)$ and $CL(A, B)$ are soft constraints that A and B must appear in the same topic, and that A and B cannot appear in the same topic, respectively.

Let us consider topic analysis of a corpus with movie reviews for illustrative purposes. We know that two words 'jackie' (means Jackie Chan) and 'kung-fu' should appear in the same topic, while 'dicaprio' (means Leonardo DiCaprio) and 'kung-fu' should not appear in the same topic. In this case, we can add constraints *ML*('jackie', 'kung-fu') and *CL*('dicaprio', 'kung-fu') to smoothly conduct analysis. However, what if there is a word 'bruce' (means Bruce Lee) in the corpus, and we want to distinguish between 'jackie' and 'bruce'? Our full knowledge among 'kung-fu', 'jackie', and 'bruce' should be (*ML*('kung-fu', 'jackie') $\vee$ *ML*('kung-fu', 'bruce')) $\wedge$ *CL*('bruce', 'jackie'), although the original framework does not allow a disjunction ($\vee$) of links. In this paper, we address such logical expressions of links on LDA-DF framework.

Combination between a probabilistic model and logical knowledge expressions such as Markov Logic Network (MLN) is recently getting a lot of attention (Riedel and Meza-Ruiz, 2008; Yu et al., 2008; Meza-Ruiz and Riedel, 2009; Yoshikawa et al., 2009; Poon and Domingos, 2009), and our work can be regarded as on this research line. At least, to our knowledge, our method is the first one that can directly incorporate logical knowledge into a prior for topic models without MLN. This means the complexity of the inference in our method is essentially the same as in the original LDA-DF, despite that our method can broaden knowledge expressions.

2 LDA with Dirichlet Forest Priors

We briefly review LDA-DF. Let $\mathbf{w} := w_1 \dots w_n$ be a corpus consisting of D documents, where n is the total number of words in the documents. Let d_i and z_i be the document that includes the i-th word w_i and the hidden topic that is assigned to w_i, respectively. Let T be the number of topics.

As in LDA, we assume a probabilistic language model that generates a corpus as a mixture of hidden topics and infer two parameters: a document-topic probability θ that represents a mixture rate of topics in each document, and a topic-word probability ϕ that represents an occurrence rate of words in each topic. The model is defined as

$$\begin{aligned} \theta_{d_i} &\sim \mathit{Dirichlet}(\alpha), \\ z_i|\theta_{d_i} &\sim \mathit{Multinomial}(\theta_{d_i}), \\ \mathbf{q} &\sim \mathit{DirichletForest}(\beta, \eta), \\ \phi_{z_i} &\sim \mathit{DirichletTree}(\mathbf{q}), \\ w_i|z_i, \phi_{z_i} &\sim \mathit{Multinomial}(\phi_{z_i}), \end{aligned}$$

where α and (β, η) are hyper parameters for θ and ϕ, respectively. The only difference between LDA and LDA-DF is that ϕ is chosen not from the Dirichlet distribution, but from the Dirichlet tree distribution (Dennis III, 1991), which is a generalization of the Dirichlet distribution. The Dirichlet forest distribution assigns one tree to each topic from a set of Dirichlet trees, into which we encode domain knowledge. The trees assigned to topics $\mathbf{z}$ are denoted as $\mathbf{q}$.

In the framework, *ML*(A, B) is achieved by the Dirichlet tree in Fig. 1(a), which equalizes the occurrence probabilities of A and B in a topic when η is large. This tree generates probabilities with *Dirichlet*$(2\beta, \beta)$ and redistributes the probability for "2β" with *Dirichlet*$(\eta\beta, \eta\beta)$.

In the case of *CL*s, we use the following algorithm.

1. Consider a undirected graph regarding words as vertices and links *CL*(A, B) as edges between A and B.
2. Divide the graph into connected components.
3. Extract the maximal independent sets of each component.
4. Create Dirichlet trees to raise the occurrence probabilities of words corresponding to each maximal independent set.

For examples, the algorithm creates the two trees in Fig. 1(b) for the constraint *CL*$(A, B) \wedge$ *CL*(A, C). The constraint is achieved when η is large, since words in each topic are chosen from the distribution of either the left tree that zeros the occurrence probability of A, or the right tree that zeros those of B and C.

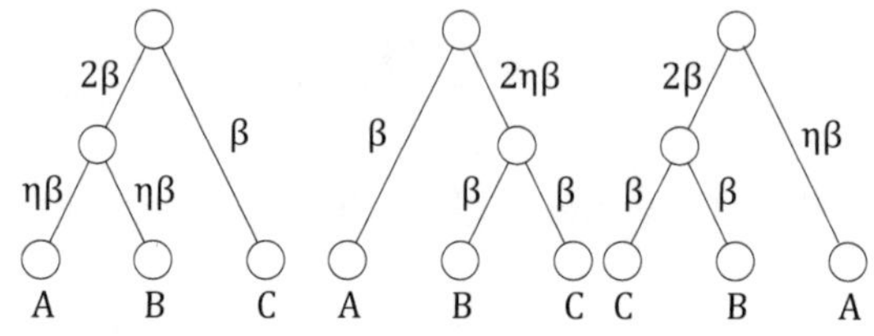

(a) *ML*(A, B) (b) *CL*$(A, B) \wedge$ *CL*(A, C)

Figure 1: Dirichlet trees for two constraints of (a) *ML*(A, B) and (b) *CL*$(A, B) \wedge$ *CL*(A, C).

Inference of ϕ and θ is achieved by alternately sampling topic z_i for each word w_i and Dirichlet tree q_z for each topic z. Since the Dirichlet tree distribution is conjugate to the multinomial distribution, the sampling equation of z_i is easily derived like LDA as follows:

$$p(z_i = z \mid \mathbf{z}_{-i}, \mathbf{q}, \mathbf{w}) \propto (n_{-i,z}^{(d_i)} + \alpha) \prod_s^{I_z(\uparrow i)} \frac{\gamma_z^{(C_z(s\downarrow i))} + n_{-i}^{(C_z(s\downarrow i))}}{\sum_k^{C_z(s)} \left(\gamma_z^{(k)} + n_{-i,z}^{(k)}\right)},$$

where $n_{-i,z}^{(d)}$ represents the number of words (excluding w_i) assigning topic z in document d. $n_{-i,z}^{(k)}$ represents the number of words (excluding w_i) assigning topic z in the subtree rooted at node k in tree q_z. $I_z(\uparrow i)$ and $C_z(s \downarrow i)$ represents the set of internal nodes and the immediate child of node s, respectively, on the path from the root to leaf w_i in tree q_z. $C_z(s)$ represents the set of children of node s in tree q_z. $\gamma_z^{(k)}$ represents a weight of the edge to node k in tree q_z. Additionally, we define $\sum_s^S := \sum_{s \in S}$.

Sampling of tree q_z is achieved by sequentially sampling subtree $q_z^{(r)}$ corresponding to the r-th connected component by using the following equation:

$$p(q_z^{(r)} = q' \mid \mathbf{z}, \mathbf{q}_{-z}, q_z^{(-r)}, \mathbf{w}) \propto |M_{r,q'}| \times \prod_s^{I_{z,r}^{(q')}} \left(\frac{\Gamma\left(\sum_k^{C_z(s)} \gamma_z^{(k)}\right) \prod_k^{C_z(s)} \Gamma\left(\gamma_z^{(k)} + n_z^{(k)}\right)}{\Gamma\left(\sum_k^{C_z(s)} (\gamma_z^{(k)} + n_z^{(k)})\right) \prod_k^{C_z(s)} \Gamma\left(\gamma_z^{(k)}\right)} \right),$$

where $I_{z,r}^{(q')}$ represents the set of internal nodes in the subtree q' corresponding to the r-th connected component for tree q_z. $|M_{r,q'}|$ represents the size of the maximal independent set corresponding to the subtree q' for r-th connected component.

After sufficiently sampling z_i and q_z, we can infer posterior probabilities $\hat{\phi}$ and $\hat{\theta}$ using the last sampled $\mathbf{z}$ and $\mathbf{q}$, in a similar manner to the standard LDA as follows.

$$\hat{\theta}_z^{(d)} = \frac{n_z^{(d)} + \alpha}{\sum_{z'=1}^{T}\left(n_{z'}^{(d)} + \alpha\right)}$$

$$\hat{\phi}_z^{(w)} = \prod_{s}^{I_z(\uparrow w)} \frac{\gamma_z^{(C_z(s\downarrow w))} + n_z^{(C_z(s\downarrow w))}}{\sum_k^{C_z(s)}\left(\gamma_z^{(k)} + n_z^{(k)}\right)}$$

3 Logical Constraints on Words

In this section, we address logical expressions of two links using disjunctions ($\vee$) and negations ($\neg$), as well as conjunctions ($\wedge$), e.g., $\neg ML(A,B) \vee ML(A,C)$. We denote it as ($\wedge$,$\vee$,$\neg$)-expressions. Since each negation can be removed in a preprocessing stage, we focus only on ($\wedge$,$\vee$)-expressions. Interpretation of negations is discussed in Sec. 3.4.

3.1 ($\wedge$,$\vee$)-expressions of Links

We propose a simple method that simultaneously achieves conjunctions and disjunctions of links, where the existing method can only treat conjunctions of links. The key observation is that any Dirichlet trees constructed by *ML*s and *CL*s are essentially based only on two primitives. One is $Ep(A,B)$ that equalizes the occurrence probabilities of A and B in a topic as in Fig. 1(a), and the other is $Np(A)$ that zeros the occurrence probability of A in a topic as in the left tree of Fig. 1(b). The right tree of Fig. 1(b) is created by $Np(B) \wedge Np(C)$. Thus, we can substitute *ML* and *CL* with *Ep* and *Np* as follows:

$$ML(A,B) = Ep(A,B)$$
$$CL(A,B) = Np(A) \vee Np(B)$$

Using this substitution, we can compile a ($\wedge$, $\vee$)-expression of links to the corresponding Dirichlet trees with the following algorithm.

1. Substitute all links (*ML* and *CL*) with the corresponding primitives (*Ep* and *Np*).
2. Calculate the minimum DNF of the primitives.
3. Construct Dirichlet trees corresponding to the (monotone) monomials of the DNF.

Let us consider three words A = 'kung-fu', B = 'jackie', and C = 'bruce' in Sec. 1. We want to constrain them with $(ML(A,B) \vee ML(A,C)) \wedge CL(B,C)$. In this case, the algorithm calculates the minimum DNF of primitives as

$$\begin{aligned}
&(ML(A,B) \vee ML(A,C)) \wedge CL(B,C) \\
&= (Ep(A,B) \vee Ep(A,C)) \wedge (Np(B) \vee Np(C)) \\
&= (Ep(A,B) \wedge Np(B)) \vee (Ep(A,B) \wedge Np(C)) \\
&\quad \vee (Ep(A,C) \wedge Np(B)) \vee (Ep(A,C) \wedge Np(C))
\end{aligned}$$

and constructs four Dirichlet trees corresponding to the four monomials $Ep(A,B) \wedge Np(B)$, $Ep(A,B) \wedge Np(C)$, $Ep(A,C) \wedge Np(B)$, and $Ep(A,C) \wedge Np(C)$ in the last equation.

Considering only ($\wedge$)-expressions of links, our method is equivalent to the existing method in the original framework in terms of an asymptotic behavior of Dirichlet trees. We define asymptotic behavior as *Asymptotic Topic Family (ATF)* as follows.

Definition 1 (Asymptotic Topic Family). *For any ($\wedge$, $\vee$)-expression f of primitives and any set $\mathcal{W}$ of words, we define* the asymptotic topic family of f with respect to $\mathcal{W}$ *as a family f^* calculated by the following rules: Given ($\wedge$, $\vee$)-expressions f_1 and f_2 of primitives and words $A, B \in \mathcal{W}$,*

$$\begin{aligned}
&\text{(i) } (f_1 \vee f_2)^* &&:= f_1^* \cup f_2^* \,, \\
&\text{(ii) } (f_1 \wedge f_2)^* &&:= f_1^* \cap f_2^* \,, \\
&\text{(iii) } Ep^*(A,B) &&:= \{\emptyset, \{A,B\}\} \otimes 2^{\mathcal{W}-\{A,B\}}, \\
&\text{(iv) } Np^*(A) &&:= 2^{\mathcal{W}-\{A\}} \,.
\end{aligned}$$

Here, notation $\otimes$ is defined as $X \otimes Y := \{x \cup y \mid x \in X, y \in Y\}$ for given two sets X and Y. ATF expresses all combinations of words that can occur in a topic when η is large. In the above example, the ATF of its expression with respect to $\mathcal{W} = \{A, B, C\}$ is calculated as

$$\begin{aligned}
&((ML(A,B) \vee ML(A,C)) \wedge CL(B,C))^* \\
&= (Ep(A,B) \vee Ep(A,C)) \wedge (Np(B) \vee Np(C))^* \\
&= \begin{pmatrix} \{\emptyset, \{A,B\}\} \otimes 2^{\mathcal{W}-\{A,B\}} \\ \cup \{\emptyset, \{A,C\}\} \otimes 2^{\mathcal{W}-\{A,C\}} \end{pmatrix} \\
&\quad \cap \left(2^{\mathcal{W}-\{B\}} \cup 2^{\mathcal{W}-\{C\}}\right) \\
&= \{\emptyset, \{B\}, \{C\}, \{A,B\}, \{A,C\}\}.
\end{aligned}$$

As we expected, the ATF of the last equation indicates such a constraint that either A and B or A and C must appear in the same topic, and B and C cannot appear in the same topic. Note that the part of $\{B\}$ satisfies $ML(A, C) \wedge CL(B, C)$. If you want to remove $\{B\}$ and $\{C\}$, you can use exclusive disjunctions. For the sake of simplicity, we omit descriptions about $\mathcal{W}$ when its instance is arbitrary or obvious from now on.

The next theorem gives the guarantee of asymptotic equivalency between our method and the existing method. Let $MIS(G)$ be the set of maximal independent sets of graph G. We define $\mathcal{L} := \{\{w, w'\} \mid w, w' \in \mathcal{W}, w \neq w'\}$. We consider *CL*s only, since the asymptotic equivalency including *ML*s is obvious by identifying all vertices connected by *ML*s.

Theorem 2. *For any $(\wedge)$-expression of CLs represented by $\bigwedge_{\{x,y\}\in\ell:\ell\subseteq\mathcal{L}} CL(x, y)$, the ATF of the corresponding minimum DNF of primitives represented by $\bigvee_{X\in\mathcal{X}:\mathcal{X}\subseteq 2^{\mathcal{W}}}(\bigwedge_{x\in X} Np(x))$ is equivalent to the union of the power sets of every maximal independent set $S \in MIS(G)$ of a graph $G := (\mathcal{W}, \ell)$, that is, $\bigcup_{X\in\mathcal{X}} (\bigcap_{x\in X} Np^*(x)) = \bigcup_{S\in MIS(G)} 2^S$.*

Proof. For any $(\wedge)$-expressions of links characterized by $\ell \subseteq \mathcal{L}$, we denote f_ℓ and G_ℓ as the corresponding minimum DNF and graph, respectively. We define $\mathcal{U}_\ell := \bigcup_{S\in MIS(G_\ell)} 2^S$. When $|\ell| = 1$, $f^*_\ell = \mathcal{U}_\ell$ is trivial. Assuming $f^*_\ell = \mathcal{U}_\ell$ when $|\ell| > 1$, for any set $\ell' := \ell \cup \{\{A, B\}\}$ with an additional link characterized by $\{A, B\} \in \mathcal{L}$, we obtain

$$
\begin{aligned}
f^*_{\ell'} &= ((Np(A) \vee Np(B)) \wedge f_\ell)^* \\
&= (2^{\mathcal{W}-\{A\}} \cup 2^{\mathcal{W}-\{B\}}) \cap \mathcal{U}_\ell \\
&= \bigcup_{S\in MIS(G_\ell)} \begin{pmatrix} (2^{\mathcal{W}-\{A\}} \cap 2^S) \\ \cup(2^{\mathcal{W}-\{B\}} \cap 2^S) \end{pmatrix} \\
&= \bigcup_{S\in MIS(G_\ell)} (2^{S-\{A\}} \cup 2^{S-\{B\}}) \\
&= \bigcup_{S\in MIS(G_{\ell'})} 2^S \quad = \quad \mathcal{U}_{\ell'}
\end{aligned}
$$

This proves the theorem by induction. In the last line of the above deformation, we used $\bigcup_{S\in MIS(G)} 2^S = \bigcup_{S\in IS(G)} 2^S$ and $MIS(G_{\ell'}) \subseteq \bigcup_{S\in MIS(G_\ell)}((S - \{A\}) \cup (S - \{B\})) \subseteq IS(G_{\ell'})$, where $IS(G)$ represents the set of all independent sets on graph G. □

In the above theorem, $\bigcup_{X\in\mathcal{X}} (\bigcap_{x\in X} Np^*(x))$ represents asymptotic behaviors of our method, while $\bigcup_{S\in MIS(G)} 2^S$ represents those of the existing method. By using a similar argument to the proof, we can prove the elements of the two sets are completely the same, i.e., $\bigcap_{x\in X} Np^*(x) = \{2^S \mid S \in MIS(G)\}$. This interestingly means that for any logical expression characterized by *CL*s, calculating its minimum DNF is the same as calculating the maximal independent sets of the corresponding graph, or the maximal cliques of its complement graph.

3.2 Shrinking Dirichlet Forests

Focusing on asymptotic behaviors, we can reduce the number of Dirichlet trees, which means the performance improvement of Gibbs sampling for Dirichlet trees. This is achieved just by minimizing DNF on *asymptotic equivalence relation* defined as follows.

Definition 3 (Asymptotic Equivalence Relation)**.** *Given two $(\wedge, \vee)$-expressions f_1, f_2, we say that f_1 is asymptotically equivalent to f_2, if and only if $f^*_1 = f^*_2$. We denote the relation as notation $\asymp$, that is, $f_1 \asymp f_2 \Leftrightarrow f^*_1 = f^*_2$.*

The next proposition gives an intuitive understanding of why asymptotic equivalence relation can shrink Dirichlet forests.

Proposition 4. *For any two words $A, B \in \mathcal{W}$,*

(a) $Ep(A, B) \vee (Np(A) \wedge Np(B)) \asymp Ep(A, B)$,

(b) $Ep(A, B) \wedge Np(A) \quad \asymp \quad Np(A) \wedge Np(B)$.

Proof. We prove (a) only.

$$
\begin{aligned}
&Ep^*(A, B) \cup (Np^*(A) \cap Np^*(B)) \\
&= \{\emptyset, \{A, B\}\} \otimes 2^{\mathcal{W}-\{A,B\}} \\
&\quad \cup (2^{\mathcal{W}-\{A\}} \cap 2^{\mathcal{W}-\{B\}}) \\
&= (\{\emptyset, \{A, B\}\} \cup (\{\emptyset, \{B\}\} \cap \{\emptyset, \{A\}\})) \\
&\quad \otimes 2^{\mathcal{W}-\{A,B\}} \\
&= \{\emptyset, \{A, B\}\} \otimes 2^{\mathcal{W}-\{A,B\}} \quad = \quad Ep^*(A, B)
\end{aligned}
$$

□

In the above proposition, Eq. (a) directly reduces the number of Dirichlet trees since a disjunction $(\vee)$ disappears, while Eq. (b) indirectly reduces since $(Np(A) \wedge Np(B)) \vee Np(B) = Np(B)$.

We conduct an experiment to clarify how many trees can be reduced by asymptotic equivalency. In the experiment, we prepare conjunctions of random links of *ML*s and *CL*s when $|\mathcal{W}| = 10$, and compare the average numbers of Dirichlet trees compiled by minimum DNF (M-DNF) and asymptotic minimum DNF (AM-DNF) in 100 trials. The experimental result shown in Tab. 1

Table 1: The average numbers of Dirichlet trees compiled by minimum DNF (M-DNF) and asymptotic minimum DNF (AM-DNF) in terms of the number of random links. Each value is the average of 100 trials.

# of links	1	2	4	8	16
M-DNF	1	2.08	3.43	6.18	10.35
AM-DNF	1	2.08	3.23	4.24	4.07

indicates that asymptotic equivalency effectively reduces the number of Dirichlet trees especially when the number of links is large.

3.3 Customizing New Links

Two primitives *Ep* and *Np* allow us to easily customize new links without changing the algorithm. Let us consider *Imply-Link*(A, B) or *IL*(A, B), which is a constraint that B must appear if A appears in a topic (informally, $A \rightarrow B$). In this case, the setting

$$\mathit{IL}(A, B) \quad = \quad \mathit{Ep}(A, B) \vee \mathit{Np}(A)$$

is acceptable, since the ATF of *IL*(A, B) with respect to $\mathcal{W} = \{A, B\}$ is $\{\emptyset, \{A, B\}, \{B\}\}$. *IL*$(A, B)$ is effective when B has multiple meanings as mentioned later in Sec. 4.

Informally regarding *IL*(A, B) as $A \rightarrow B$ and *ML*(A, B) as $A \Leftrightarrow B$, *ML*(A, B) seems to be the same meaning of *IL*$(A, B) \wedge$ *IL*(B, A). However, this anticipation is wrong on the normal equivalency, i.e., *ML*$(A, B) \neq$ *IL*$(A, B) \wedge$ *IL*(B, A). The asymptotic equivalency can fulfill the anticipation with the next proposition. This simultaneously suggests that our definition is semantically valid.

Proposition 5. *For any two words* $A, B \in \mathcal{W}$,

$$\mathit{IL}(A, B) \wedge \mathit{IL}(B, A) \quad \asymp \quad \mathit{ML}(A, B)$$

Proof. From Proposition 4,

$$\begin{aligned} & \mathit{IL}(A, B) \wedge \mathit{IL}(B, A) \\ = \quad & (\mathit{Ep}(A, B) \vee \mathit{Np}(A)) \wedge (\mathit{Ep}(B, A) \vee \mathit{Np}(B)) \\ = \quad & \mathit{Ep}(A, B) \vee (\mathit{Ep}(A, B) \wedge \mathit{Np}(A)) \\ & \vee (\mathit{Ep}(A, B) \wedge \mathit{Np}(B)) \vee (\mathit{Np}(A) \wedge \mathit{Np}(B)) \\ \asymp \quad & \mathit{Ep}(A, B) \vee (\mathit{Np}(A) \wedge \mathit{Np}(B)) \\ \asymp \quad & \mathit{Ep}(A, B) \; = \; \mathit{ML}(A, B) \end{aligned}$$

Further, we can construct *XIL*$(X_1, \cdots, X_n, Y)$ as an extended version of *IL*(A, B), which allows us to use multiple conditions like Horn clauses. This informally means $\bigwedge_{i=1}^{n} X_i \rightarrow Y$ as an extension of $A \rightarrow B$. In this case, we set

$$\mathit{XIL}(X_1, \cdots, X_n, Y) = \bigwedge_{i=1}^{n} \mathit{Ep}(X_i, Y) \vee \bigvee_{i=1}^{n} \mathit{Np}(X_i).$$

When we want to isolate unnecessary words (i.e., stop words), we can use *Isolate-Link* (*ISL*) defined as

$$\mathit{ISL}(X_1, \cdots, X_n) \quad = \quad \bigwedge_{i=1}^{n} \mathit{Np}(X_i).$$

This is easier than considering *CL*s between high-frequency words and unnecessary words as described in (Andrzejewski et al., 2009).

3.4 Negation of Links

There are two types of interpretation for negation of links. One is *strong negation*, which regards $\neg$*ML*(A, B) as "A and B must not appear in the same topic", and the other is *weak negation*, which regards it as "A and B need not appear in the same topic". We set $\neg$*ML*$(A, B) \asymp$ *CL*(A, B) for strong negation, while we just remove $\neg$*ML*(A, B) for weak negation. We consider the strong negation in this study.

According to Def. 1, the ATF of the negation $\neg f$ of primitive f seems to be defined as $(\neg f)^* := 2^{\mathcal{W}} - f^*$. However, this definition is not fit in strong negation, since $\neg$*ML*$(A, B) \not\asymp$ *CL*(A, B) on the definition. Thus we define it to be fit in strong negation as follows.

Definition 6 (ATF of strong negation of links)**.** *Given a link* L *with arguments* $X_1, \cdots, X_n$, *letting* f_L *be the primitives of* L, *we define the ATF of the negation of* L *as* $(\neg L(X_1, \cdots, X_n))^* := (2^{\mathcal{W}} - f_L^*(X_1, \cdots, X_n)) \cup 2^{\mathcal{W} - \{X_1, \cdots, X_n\}}$.

Note that the definition is used not for primitives but for links. Actually, the similar definition for primitives is not fit in strong negation, and so we must remove all negations in a preprocessing stage.

The next proposition gives the way to remove the negation of each link treated in this study. We define no constraint condition as ϵ for the result of *ISL*.

Proposition 7. *For any words* $A, B, X_1, \cdots, X_n$, $Y \in \mathcal{W}$,

(a) $\neg ML(A, B) \asymp CL(A, B)$,

(b) $\neg CL(A, B) \asymp ML(A, B)$,

(c) $\neg IL(A, B) \asymp Np(B)$,

(d) $\neg XIL(X_1, \cdots, X_n, Y)$
$\asymp \bigwedge_{i=1}^{n-1} Ep(X_i, X_n) \wedge Np(Y)$,

(e) $\neg ISL(X_1, \cdots, X_n) \asymp \epsilon$.

Proof. We prove (a) only.

$$\begin{aligned}
&(\neg ML(A, B))^* \\
&= (2^{\mathcal{W}} - Ep^*(A, B)) \cup 2^{\mathcal{W}-\{A,B\}} \\
&= (2^{\{A,B\}} - \{\emptyset, \{A, B\}\}) \otimes 2^{\mathcal{W}-\{A,B\}} \\
&\qquad \cup 2^{\mathcal{W}-\{A,B\}} \\
&= \{\emptyset, \{A\}, \{B\}\} \otimes 2^{\mathcal{W}-\{A,B\}} \\
&= 2^{\mathcal{W}-\{A\}} \cup 2^{\mathcal{W}-\{B\}} \\
&= Np^*(A) \cup Np^*(B) \quad = \quad (CL(A, B))^*
\end{aligned}$$

□

4 Comparison on a Synthetic Corpus

We experiment using a synthetic corpus $\{ABAB, ACAC\} \times 2$ with vocabulary $\mathcal{W} = \{A, B, C\}$ to clarify the property of our method in the same way as in the existing work (Andrzejewski et al., 2009). We set topic size as $T = 2$. The goal of this experiment is to obtain two topics: a topic where A and B frequently occur and a topic where A and C frequently occur. We abbreviate the grouping type as $AB|AC$. In preliminary experiments, LDA yielded almost four grouping types: $AB|AC$, $AB|C$, $AC|B$, and $A|BC$. Thus, we naively classify a grouping type of each result into the four types. Concretely speaking, for any two topic-word probabilities $\hat{\phi}$ and $\hat{\phi}'$, we calculate the average of Euclidian distances between each vector component of $\hat{\phi}$ and the corresponding one of $\hat{\phi}'$, ignoring the difference of topic labels, and regard them as the same type if the average is less than 0.1.

Fig. 2 shows the occurrence rates of grouping types on 1,000 results after 1,000 iterations by LDA-DF with six constraints (1) no constraint, (2) $ML(A, B)$, (3) $CL(B, C)$, (4) $ML(A, B) \wedge CL(B, C)$, (5) $IL(B, A)$, and (6) $ML(A, B) \vee ML(A, C)$. In the experiment, we set $\alpha = 1$, $\beta = 0.01$, and $\eta = 100$. In the figure, the higher rate of the objective type $AB|AC$ (open bar) is better. The results of (1-4) can be achieved even by the existing method, and those of (5-6) can be achieved only by our method. Roughly speaking, the figure shows that our method is clearly better than the existing method, since our method can obtain almost 100% as the rate of $AB|AC$, which is the best of all results, while the existing methods can only obtain about 60%, which is the best of the results of (1-4).

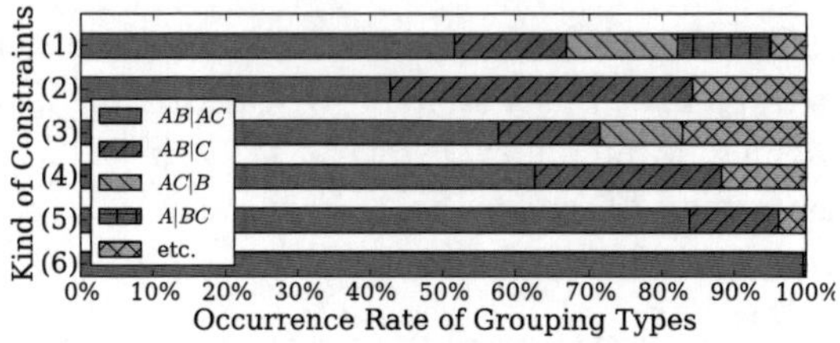

Figure 2: Rates of Grouping types in the 1,000 results on synthetic corpus $\{ABAB, ACAC\} \times 2$ with six constraints: (1) no constraint, (2) $ML(A, B)$, (3) $CL(B, C)$, (4) $ML(A, B) \wedge CL(B, C)$, (5) $IL(B, A)$, and (6) $ML(A, B) \vee ML(A, C)$.

The result of (1) is the same result as LDA, because of no constraints. In the result, the rate of $AB|AC$ is only about 50%, since each of $AB|C$, $AC|B$, and $A|BC$ remains at a high 15%. As we expected, the result of (2) shows that $ML(A, B)$ cannot remove $AB|C$ although it can remove $AC|B$ and $A|BC$, while the result of (3) shows that $CL(B, C)$ cannot remove $AB|C$ and $AC|B$ although it can remove $A|BC$. The result of (4) indicates that $ML(A, B) \wedge CL(B, C)$ is the best of knowledge expressions in the existing method. Note that $ML(A, B) \wedge ML(A, C)$ implies $ML(B, C)$ by transitive law and is inconsistent with all of the four types. The result (80%) of (5) $IL(B, A)$ is interestingly better than that (60%) of (4), despite that (5) has less primitives than (4). The reason is that (5) allows A to appear with C, while (4) does not. In the result of (6) $ML(A, B) \vee ML(A, C)$, the constraint achieves almost 100%, which is the best of knowledge expressions in our method. Of course, the constraint of $(ML(A, B) \vee ML(A, C)) \wedge CL(B, C)$ can also achieve almost 100%.

5 Interactive Topic Analysis

We demonstrate advantages of our method via interactive topic analysis on a real corpus, which consists of stemmed, down-cased 1,000 (positive) movie reviews used in (Pang and Lee, 2004). In this experiment, the parameters are set as $\alpha = 1$, $\beta = 0.01$, $\eta = 1000$, and $T = 20$.

We first ran LDA-DF with 1,000 iterations without any constraints and noticed that most topics have stop words (e.g., 'have' and 'not') and corpus-specific, unnecessary words (e.g., 'film', 'movie'), as in the first block in Tab. 2. To remove them, we added *ISL*('film', 'movie', 'have', 'not', 'n't') to the constraint of LDA-DF, which is compiled to one Dirichlet tree. After the second run of LDA-DF with the isolate-link, we specified most topics such as Comedy, Disney, and Family, since cumbersome words are isolated, and so we noticed that two topics about Star Wars and Star Trek are merged, as in the second block. Each topic label is determined by looking carefully at high-frequency words in the topic. To split the merged two topics, we added *CL*('jedi', 'trek') to the constraint, which is compiled to two Dirichlet trees. However, after the third run of LDA-DF, we noticed that there is no topic only about Star Trek, since 'star' appears only in the Star Wars topic, as in the third block. Note that the topic including 'trek' had other topics such as a topic about comedy film Big Lebowski. We finally added *ML*('star', 'jedi') $\vee$ *ML*('star', 'trek') to the constraint, which is compiled to four Dirichlet trees, to split the two topics considering polysemy of 'star'. After the fourth run of LDA-DF, we appropriately obtained two topics about Star Wars and Star Trek as in the fourth block. Note that our solution is not ad-hoc, and we can easily apply it to similar problems.

Table 2: Characteristic topics obtained in the experiment on the real corpus. Four blocks in the table corresponds to the results of the four constraints ϵ, *ISL*($\cdots$), *CL*('jedi', 'trek') $\wedge$ *ISL*($\cdots$), and (*ML*('jedi', 'trek') $\vee$ *ML*('star', 'trek')) $\wedge$ *CL*('jedi', 'trek') $\wedge$ *ISL*($\cdots$), respectively.

Topic	High frequency words in each topic
?	**have** give night **film** turn performance
?	**not** life **have** own first only family tell
?	**movie have n't** get good **not** see
?	**have** black scene tom death die joe
?	**film have n't not** make out well see
Isolated	**have film movie not** good make **n't**
?	**star** war trek planet effect special
Comedy	comedy funny laugh school hilarious
Disney	disney voice mulan animated song
Family	life love family mother woman father
Isolated	**have film movie not** make good **n't**
StarWars	**star** war lucas effect jedi special
?	science world trek fiction lebowski
Comedy	funny comedy laugh get hilarious
Disney	disney truman voice toy show
Family	family father mother boy child son
Isolated	**have film movie not** make good **n't**
StarWars	**star** war toy jedi menace phantom
StarTrek	alien effect **star** science special trek
Comedy	comedy funny laugh hilarious joke
Disney	disney voice animated mulan
Family	life love family man story child

6 Conclusions

We proposed a simple method to achieve topic models with logical constraints on words. Our method compiles a given constraint to the prior of LDA-DF, which is a recently developed semi-supervised extension of LDA with Dirichlet forest priors. As well as covering the constraints in the original LDA-DF, our method allows us to construct new customized constraints without changing the algorithm. We proved that our method is asymptotically the same as the existing method for any constraints with conjunctive expressions, and showed that asymptotic equivalency can shrink a constructed Dirichlet forest. In the comparative study on a synthetic corpus, we clarified the property of our method, and in the interactive topic analysis on a movie review corpus, we demonstrated its effectiveness. In the future, we intend to address detail comparative studies on real corpora and consider a simple method integrating negations into a whole, although we removed them in a preprocessing stage in this study.

References

David Andrzejewski and Xiaojin Zhu. 2009. Latent Dirichlet Allocation with Topic-in-Set Knowledge. In *Proceedings of the NAACL HLT 2009 Workshop on Semi-Supervised Learning for Natural Language Processing*, pages 43–48.

David Andrzejewski, Anne Mulhern, Ben Liblit, and Xiaojin Zhu. 2007. Statistical Debugging Using Latent Topic Models. In *Proceedings of the 18th European Conference on Machine Learning (ECML 2007)*, pages 6–17. Springer-Verlag.

David Andrzejewski, Xiaojin Zhu, and Mark Craven. 2009. Incorporating domain knowledge into topic modeling via Dirichlet Forest priors. In *Proceedings of the 26th Annual International Conference on Machine Learning (ICML 2009)*, pages 25–32. ACM.

Sugato Basu, Ian Davidson, and Kiri Wagstaff. 2008. *Constrained Clustering: Advances in Algorithms, Theory, and Applications*. Chapman & Hall/CRC, 1 edition.

David M. Blei, Andrew Y. Ng, and Michael I. Jordan. 2003. Latent Dirichlet Allocation. *Journal of Machine Learning Research*, 3:993–1022.

Samuel Y. Dennis III. 1991. On the hyper-Dirichlet type 1 and hyper-Liouville distributions. *Communications in Statistics — Theory and Methods*, 20(12):4069–4081.

Ivan Meza-Ruiz and Sebastian Riedel. 2009. Jointly Identifying Predicates, Arguments and Senses using Markov Logic. In *Proceedings of Human Language Technologies: The 2009 Annual Conference of the North American Chapter of the Association for Computational Linguistics (NAACL HLT 2009)*, pages 155–163. Association for Computational Linguistics.

Bo Pang and Lillian Lee. 2004. A Sentimental Education: Sentiment Analysis Using Subjectivity Summarization Based on Minimum Cuts. In *Proceedings of the 42nd Annual Meeting on Association for Computational Linguistics (ACL 2004)*, pages 271–278.

Hoifung Poon and Pedro Domingos. 2009. Unsupervised Semantic Parsing. In *Proceedings of the 2009 Conference on Empirical Methods in Natural Language Processing (EMNLP 2009)*, pages 1–10. Association for Computational Linguistics.

Sebastian Riedel and Ivan Meza-Ruiz. 2008. Collective Semantic Role Labelling with Markov Logic. In *Proceedings of the 12th Conference on Computational Natural Language Learning (CoNLL 2008)*, pages 193–197. Association for Computational Linguistics.

Kristina Toutanova and Mark Johnson. 2008. A Bayesian LDA-based model for semi-supervised part-of-speech tagging. In *Advances in Neural Information Processing Systems 20*, pages 1521–1528. MIT Press.

Katsumasa Yoshikawa, Sebastian Riedel, Masayuki Asahara, and Yuji Matsumoto. 2009. Jointly Identifying Temporal Relations with Markov Logic. In *Proceedings of the Joint Conference of the 47th Annual Meeting of the Association for Computational Linguistics and the 4th International Joint Conference on Natural Language Processing of the Asian Federation of Natural Language Processing (ACL-IJCNLP 2009)*, pages 405–413. Association for Computational Linguistics.

Xiaofeng Yu, Wai Lam, and Shing-Kit Chan. 2008. A Framework Based on Graphical Models with Logic for Chinese Named Entity Recognition. In *Proceedings of the 3rd International Joint Conference on Natural Language Processing (IJCNLP 2008)*, pages 335–342.

Investigation of Co-training Views and Variations for Semantic Role Labeling

Rasoul Samad Zadeh Kaljahi
Department of AI, FCSIT
University Malaya, Malaysia
research@rasulsk.info

Mohd Sapiyan Baba
Department of AI, FCSIT
University Malaya, Malaysia
pian@um.edu.my

Abstract

Co-training, as a semi-supervised learning method, has been recently applied to semantic role labeling to reduce the need for costly annotated data using unannotated data. A main concern in co-training is how to split the problem into multiple views to derive learning features, so that they can effectively train each other. We investigate various feature splits based on two SRL views, constituency and dependency, with different variations of the algorithm. Balancing the feature split in terms of the performance of the underlying classifiers showed to be useful. Also, co-training with a common training set performed better than when separate training sets are used for co-trained classifiers.

1 Introduction

Semantic role labeling (SRL) parses a natural language sentence into its event structure. This information has been shown useful for several NLP tasks such as information extraction, question answering, summarization, and machine translation (Surdeanu et al., 2003; Gimenez and Marquez, 2008).

After its introduction by Gildea and Jurafsky (2002), a considerable body of NLP research has been devoted to SRL. CoNLL 2004 and 2005 (Carreras and Marquez, 2004; 2005) followed that seminal work by using similar input resources mainly built upon *constituent-based syntax* and achieved state-of-the-art results (Koomen et al., 2005). Subsequent CoNLL shared tasks (Surdeanu et al., 2008) put forth the use of another framework based on *dependency syntax*. This framework also led to well-performed systems (Johansson and Nugues, 2008).

Almost all of the SRL research has been based on supervised machine learning methods exploiting manually annotated corpora like FrameNet (Baker et al., 1998) and PropBank (Palmer et al., 2005). FrameNet annotates some example sentences for each *semantic frame*, which questions its representativeness of the language, necessary for statistical learning. Propbank, on the other hand, annotates all the sentences from WSJ corpus and remedies that problem to some extent, but unlike FrameNet, its coverage is limited to the newswire text of WSJ.

This domain dependence affects the performance of the systems using PropBank on any different domain of text (Carreras and Marquez, 2005). Considering the cost and difficulty of creating such resources with all of these shortcomings, it seems infeasible to build a comprehensive hand-crafted corpus of natural language for training robust SRL systems.

Such issues in statistical learning have motivated researchers to devise *semi-supervised* learning methods. These methods aim at utilizing a large amount of unannotated data along with small amount of annotated data. The existence of raw natural text in huge amounts is a promising point of using such methods for SRL.

Co-training is a semi-supervised algorithm in which two or more classifiers iteratively provide each other with the training examples by labeling unannotated data. Each classifier is based on the learning features derived from *conditionally independent* and *redundant* views of the underlying problem. These two assumptions are stated as the requirements of the algorithm in its original work by Blum and Mitchell (1998).

Constituency and dependency provide attractive views of SRL problem to be exploited in a co-training setup. The major motivation is the promising results of their use in SRL, which satisfies the first assumption. There is a set of rules to convert constituency to dependency (Johansson and Nugues, 2007), which may question the second assumption. However, these rules are one-way, and moreover, Abney (2002) argues that this assumption can be loosened.

While several parameters are involved in co-training of SRL systems, the most important one is the split of the feature views. This work investigates the effects of feature split by comparing the co-training progress when using various splits. It also examines several variations of the algorithm. The algorithm is applied to the SRL problem when only a small amount of labeled data is available.

2 Related Work

Co-training was originally proposed by Blum and Mitchell (1998) for the problem of web page classification. They used hyper links pointing to the sample web page as one view and the content of the web page as another view to derive learning features. They could reduce the error rate of the base supervised classifier by co-training with unlabeled web pages.

Motivated by these results, the algorithm was applied to other NLP domains, ranging from binary classification problems like text classification (Nigam and Ghani, 2000) and reference resolution (Ng and Cardie, 2003) to more complex problems like parsing (Sarkar, 2001) and POS tagging (Clark et al., 2003). Some compared co-training with other semi-supervised algorithms like self-training and some studied variations of the algorithm for adapting it to the underlying problem. Whereas some of them reported successful results (Sarkar, 2001), some others preferred other algorithms over it (Ng and Cardie, 2003) or suggested further needs for studying the algorithm due to the large scale of the target problem (Pierce and Cardie, 2001).

Besides few other approaches to semi-supervised learning of SRL (Furstenau and Lapata, 2009), two works investigated the co-training algorithm for SRL.

He and Gildea (2006) addressed the problem of unseen FrameNet frames by using co-training (and self-training). They used syntactic and lexical views of the problem as two co-training views. They used only *tree path* as the syntactic and *head word form* as lexical features. To reduce the complexity of the task, they generalized argument roles to 15 thematic roles. The big performance gap between the two classifiers, unbalanced class distribution over examples, and the complexity of the task were argued as the reasons of the poor results.

Lee et al. (2007) investigated the utility of unlabeled data in amplifying the performance of SRL system. They trained Maximum Entropy classifiers on PropBank data as the base classifiers and used co-training to utilize a huge amount of unlabeled data (7 times more than labeled seed). The feature split they employed were the same as previous work, except they used more features for each view and also some features common between the views.

Unlike He and Gildea (2006) that used separate training sets for each classifier, they used a common training set. They only addressed core arguments to manage the complexity. Again, the performance gap between two views were high (~19 F1 points), but it is not clear why they reported the co-training results with the performance of all features instead of that of each view. They attributed the little gain to the low performance of the base classifiers and inadequacy of unlabeled data.

3 The SRL System

In order to be able to employ constituency and dependency features for two co-training views, we developed a two-platform SRL system: constituent-based and dependency-based.

One important issue in co-training of these two different platforms is that sample granularity in constituent-based system is a Penn tree constituent and in the dependency-based system is a dependency relation or a word token. Converting these to each other is necessary for co-training. Previous work (Hacioglu, 2004) shows that this conversion is not straightforward and negatively affect the performance.

To treat this issue we base our sample generation on constituency and then derive one dependency-based sample from every constituent-based sample. This sample is a word token (called *argument word* here), selected from among all word tokens inside the constituent using the heuristic used for preparing CoNLL 2008 shared task data (Surdeanu et al. 2008). This one-to-one relation is recorded in the system and helps avoid the conversion flaw. The system is described here.

Architecture: A three-stage pipeline architecture is used, where in the first stage less-probable argument candidates in the constituency parse tree are *pruned* using Xue and Palmer (2004) algorithm. In the next stage, final arguments are *identified* and *assigned* a semantic role jointly to decrease the complexity of task. In the final stage, a simple *global optimization* is performed using two constraints: a core argument role cannot be *repeated* for a predicate and arguments of a predicate cannot *overlap*. In addition, a preprocessing stage identifies the verb predicates of unlabeled sentences based on the parser's POS tags.

Features: Appendix A lists the learning features. Three types of features are used: constituent-based (C), dependency-based (D), and general (G) features which are not dependent on constituency or dependency. Columns 1 to 4 determine the feature sets and features present in each set, which will be described in the experiments section. We have tried to avoid features like named entity tags to depend less on extra annotation.

Classifier: *Maximum Entropy* is chosen as the base classifier for both views, because of its efficiency in training time and also its built-in multi-classification capability. Furthermore, it assigns a probability score for its predictions, which is useful in training data selection process in co-training. The *Maxent Toolkit*[1] is interfaced with the system for this purpose.

4 Co-training

Since the introduction of the original co-training algorithm, several variations of it have been used. These variants have usually been motivated by the characteristics of the underlying application. Figure 1 shows a generalized version of the algorithm with highlighted variables which constitute different versions of it. Some of the parameters addressed in this work are described here.

One important factor involved in bootstrapping is the performance of the base classifier (**C1** and **C2**). In co-training, another interesting parameter is the relative performance of the classifiers. We are interested in this parameter and investigate it by varying the feature split.

There are various stop criteria (**S**) used in literature, such as a pre-determined number of iterations, finishing all of the unlabeled data, or convergence of the process in terms of improvement. We use the second option for all experiments here, but we also look at convergence so that some data does not cause infinite loop.

In each iteration, one can label all of the unlabeled data or select and load a number of unlaleled examples (**p**) into a *pool* (**P**) and label

1- Add the seed example set ***L*** to currently empty training sets ***T1*** and ***T2***.
2- Train the base classifiers ***C1*** and ***C2*** with training sets ***T1*** and ***T2*** respectively.
3- Iterate the following steps until the stop criterion ***S*** is met.
  a- **Select** ***p*** examples from ***U*** into pool ***P***.
  b- Label pool ***P*** with classifiers ***C1*** and ***C2***
  c- **Select** ***n*** labeled examples whose score meets a certain threshold ***t*** from ***P*** and **add** to training sets ***T1*** and ***T2***.
  d- Retrain the classifiers ***C1*** and ***C2*** with new training sets.

Figure 1: Generalized Co-training Algorithm

only them. To study the effect of all parameters in a step by step approach, we do not use pool in this work and leave it for the future.

Selecting the newly labeled data to be **added** to the training set is the crucial point of co-training. First, it should be determined that both views use the *common* or *separate* training set during co-training. In the former case, ***T1*** and ***T2*** are identical. Then, it should be decided how the classifiers collaborate with each other.

With a common training set, selection can be done based on the prediction of both classifiers together. In one approach, only samples with the same predicted labels by both classifiers are selected (*agreement-based* selection). Another way is to select the most confidently labeled samples. Some select the most confident labelings from each view (Blum and Mitchell, 1998). In this method, a sample may be selected by both views, so this conflict needs to be resolved. We select the label for a sample with the highest confidence among both views (*confidenece-based* selection) to avoid conflict. Both approaches are investigated here.

With a separate trainings set, selection is done among samples labeled by each classifier individually (usually confidence-based). In this case, selected samples of one view are added to the training set of the other for collaboration. We are interetsed in the comparison of common and separate training sets, especially because from the two previous SRL co-training works, one was based on common (Lee et al., 2007) and the other on separate training sets (He and Gildea, 2006).

The next step is to chose the selection criteria. One can select all of the labeled examples, or one can only select a number of them (**n**), known as *growth size*, often based on a quality measure

[1]http://homepages.inf.ed.ac.uk/lzhang10/maxent_toolkit.html

F.S.	Synt. Input	All Labeled Training Data						Seed Training Data					
		WSJ Test			Brown Test			WSJ Test			Brown Test		
		P	R	F1	P	R	F1	P	R	F1	P	R	F1
1	cha	79.0	67.6	**72.9**	70.4	56.6	**62.7**	73.9	62.9	**68.0**	66.6	52.4	**58.6**
	cha.re*	79.3	73.4	**76.2**	68.6	60.8	**64.4**	75.6	68.8	**72.0**	65.1	56.1	**60.2**
2	malt	74.4	55.1	**63.3**	67.3	46.4	**55.0**	69.6	51.7	**59.4**	63.1	44.1	**51.9**
	conv*	75.5	60.8	**67.4**	69.7	52.9	**60.1**	73.6	56.9	**64.2**	66.0	47.7	**55.4**
3	cha	70.4	63.0	**66.5**	62.1	52.2	**56.8**	64.0	59.4	**61.6**	57.5	49.5	**53.2**
	cha.re*	71.2	68.8	**70.0**	68.6	60.8	**64.4**	70.4	64.3	**67.2**	60.7	53.3	**56.7**
4	malt	75.3	58.3	**65.7**	68.3	49.6	**57.5**	71.9	54.5	**62.0**	65.4	46.4	**54.2**
	conv*	76.6	64.5	**70.0**	69.7	52.9	**60.1**	76.3	59.5	**66.9**	69.0	49.8	**57.9**

Table 1: Performance of the Base Classifiers with Various Syntactic Inputs and Feature Sets

such as labeling confidence. To prevent poor relabelings diminishing the quality of the training set, a threshold (**t**) is also set on this measure. We select all labeled samples here.

Finally, when adding the selected samples into the training set, a copy of them can be kept in the unlabeled data set and labeled again in the successive iterations, or all can be removed so that each sample is labeled only once. The former is called *delibility* and the latter *indelibility* (Abney 2008). We use the second method here.

5 Experiments and Results

This work uses co-training to address the SRL training problem when the amount of available annotated data is small.

The data and evaluation settings used are similar to the CoNLL 2005 and 2008 shared tasks. For evaluation, the same script used for 2005 shared task is used here and the measures are *precision*, *recall*, and their harmonic mean, *F1*. However, the data is changed in some ways to fulfill the objectives of this research, which is explained in the next section.

5.1 The Data

All the training data including labeled and unlabeled are selected from training sections of the shared tasks which consist of 39,832 PropBank sentences. The development data is WSJ section 24 of the PropBank, and the test data is WSJ section 23. Also, the Brown test data is used to evaluate the generalization ability of the system.

As syntactic input for the constituent-based system, training and test sentences were reparsed with the reranking parser of Charniak and Johnson (2005) instead of using the original parses of the shared task. The reason was a significant improvement of the SRL performance using the new parses in the preliminary experiments. These results are given in the next section for comparison.

For dependency-based system, the dependency syntax was prepared by converting the above constituent-based parses to dependency parses using the LTH converter (Johansson and Nugues, 2007). It should be noted that the data were also parsed using MaltParser (Nivre et al. 2007) at the same time, but the converter-based system outperformed it. These results are given in the next section for comparison.

As labeled seed data, 4,000 sentence of the training sentences are selected randomly. These sentences contain 70,345 argument samples covering 38 semantic roles out of 52 roles present in the total training set. Unlike previous work, we address all core and adjunctive roles.

As unlabeled training data, we use the remaining portion of the training data which contains 35,832 sentences, including 672,672 argument samples. We only address verb predicates and automatically identify them for unlabeled sentences instead of using the original predicate annotation of the data.

5.2 The Base Classifiers

Table 1 shows the performance of the base classifiers with different feature sets presented in section 3, and different syntactic input for each feature set. The first column lists the feature set numbers. In the second column, *cha* stands for the original Charniak parses of the data, and *cha.re* stands for the reranking parser used in this work. Also, *conv* stands for the converter-based dependency syntax and *malt* for dependency syntax produced by MaltParser. Those marked with * will be used here. Precision and recall are shown by *P* and *R* respectively.

To compare the performance of the classifiers with previous work, the results with all labeled data (39,832 sentences) are given on the left; to the right are the results with seed data only (4000 labeled sentences).

5.3 Feature Splits

We experimented with three kinds of feature splits. The first feature split (UBUS) uses feature sets 1 and 4. It is neither balanced nor separated: there is 5.2 and 2.4 points F_1 gap between their classifiers on WSJ and Brown test sets respectively (see Table 1, Seed Training Data, rows 2 and 8 of the result values), and they have 4 general features in common (See Appendix A). The idea behind this feature split is to understand the impact of feature separation and balancing.

The second one (UBS) consists of feature sets 1 and 2. According to Table 1 (Seed Training Data, rows 2 and 4 of the result values), there is a bigger F_1 gap between two classifiers (~8 and ~5 points on WSJ and Brown respectively) than previous split. Thus the classifiers are still *unbalanced*. However, it is a *separated* split, since there is no features common between feature sets.

The last split (BS) is also a *separated* split but has been *balanced* by moving all general features except predicate's POS tag into the dependency-based feature set. It consists of feature sets 3 and 4. According to Table 1 (Seed Training Data, rows 6 and 8 of the result values), the balance is only on F1 and gaps exist between precision and recall in opposite directions, which roughly compensate each other.

These three feature splits are used with three variations of the co-training algorithms described in section 4. In all settings, no pool is used and all unlabeled data are labeled in each iteration. Any sample which meets the selection criteria is selected and moved to training set (indelibility), i.e., no growth size and probability threshold is specified. The results are presented and discussed in the following sections.

5.4 Co-training by Common Training Set

Two variations of the algorithm, when using a common training set, are used and described here.

Agreement-based Selection: In each iteration, any sample for which the same label is assigned by both classifiers is selected and moved into training set. Figures 2 to 7 show the results with this setting. The left and right side figures are the results on WSJ Brown test sets respectively. Precision, recall, and F_1 are plotted for the classifier of each feature set as co-training progresses. The F_1 of the base classifiers and best co-trained classifier (in case of improvement) are marked on the graphs. Horizontal axis is based on co-training iterations, but the labels are the amounts of training samples used in each iteration.

It is also apparent that the dependency-based classifier is benefitting more from co-training. The reason may be twofold. First, with all splits, it has a higher precision than the other, which helps reduce noise propagation into the subsequent iterations. Next, with unbalanced splits (1 and 3) its performance is much lower and there is more room for improvement.

All the figures show an improvement on Brown test set. Seemingly, since this test set suffers from unseen events more than the other test set, new data is more useful for it.

Most of the unlabeled data (~90%) is added in the first iteration, showing a high level of agreement between classifiers.

Figure 2 shows that there is no improvement by co-training with feature set UBUS on WSJ test set over the baseline, though the dependency-based classifier improves. The feature split UBS in Figure 4, which fully separates the two feature sets, also could not gain any benefit. It seems that separating feature sets is not effective with the presence of a large gap between classifiers. This is further confirmed by observing the results for feature split BS in Figure 6, where the gap has been decreased to 0.4 F_1 points, and co-training could improve the baseline by 0.7 points.

Although these improvements are slight, but more runs of the experiments with different random selections of seed and unlabeled data showed a consistent behavior.

Confidence-based Selection: Due to the nature of this kind of selection and since there is no growth size and probability criteria, all samples are added to the training set at once, with a label that its classifier is more confident than the other's. Therefore, instead in a chart, the results could be presented in a table (Table 2). The first column lists the feature splits. In the second column, 0 stands for the base classifier and 1 is for classifier of the first (and the only) iteration.

Using all data at once leads to an overall final classifiers performance, unlike the previous setting in which remaining data for the following iterations degraded the progress.

Considering the high level of agreement between classifiers (%90), a similar behavior to agreement-based method is observed with this method as expected. The trend of precision and recall, more improvement of dependency-based classifier, and better results on Brown test set are consistent with agreement-based co-training.

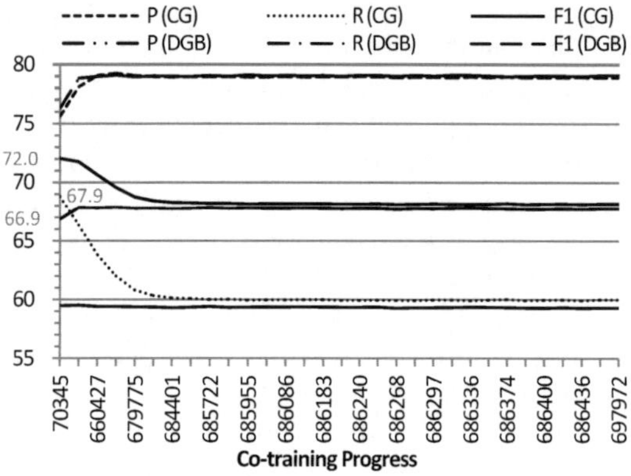

Figure 2: Agreement-based Co-training with Feature Split UBUS (WSJ Test Set)

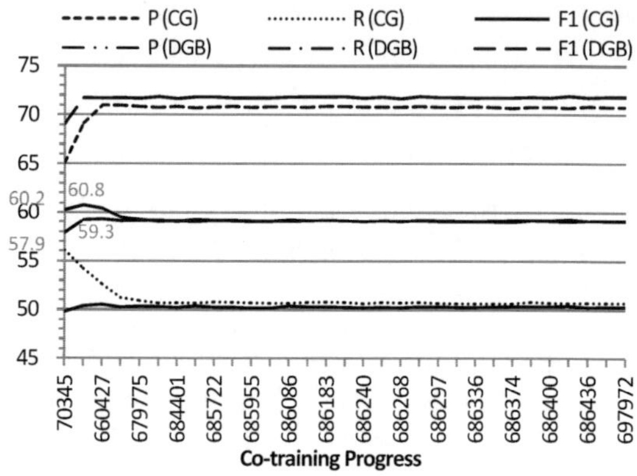

Figure 3: Agreement-based Co-training with Feature Split UBUS (Brown Test Set)

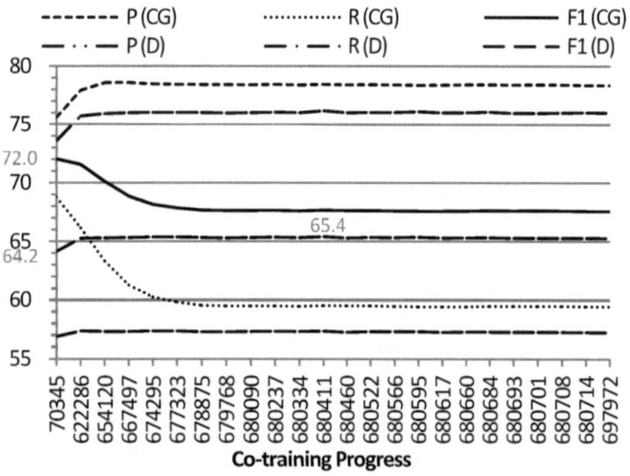

Figure 4: Agreement-based Co-training with Feature Split UBS (WSJ Test Set)

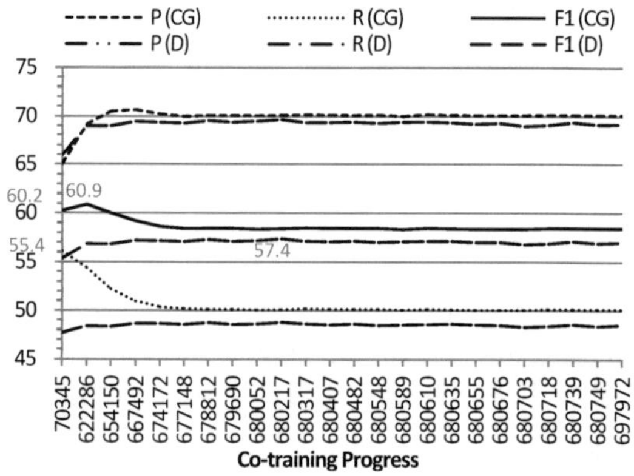

Figure 5: Agreement-based Co-training with Feature Split UBS (Brown Test Set)

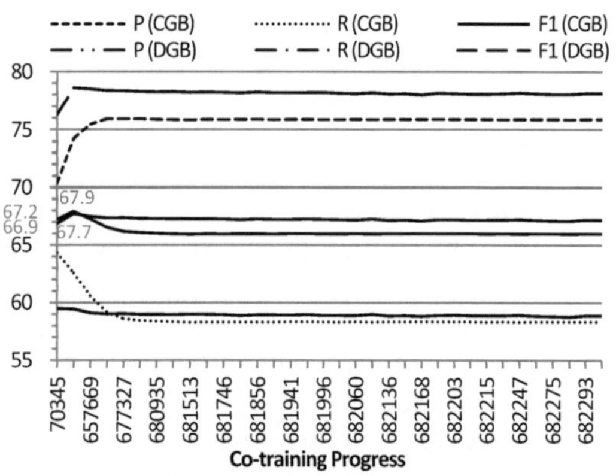

Figure 6: Agreement-based Co-training with Feature Split BS (WSJ Test Set)

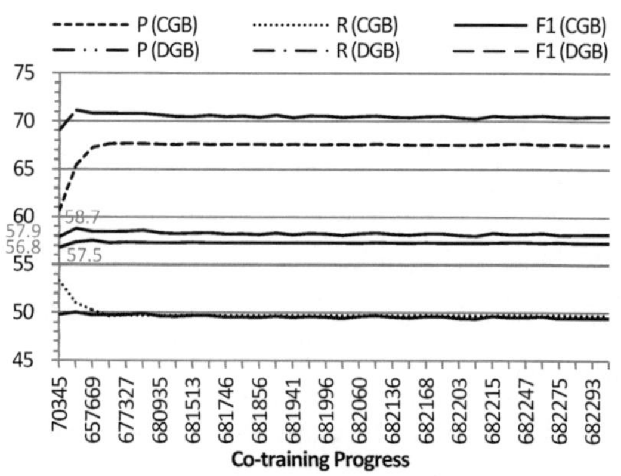

Figure 7: Agreement-based Co-training with Feature Split BS (Brown Test Set)

However, the separation of feature sets has even degraded the results over UBUS (71.2 vs. 71.8 and 59.8 vs. 60.5 F_1 points), but balancing has been again useful and improved the baselines by 0.4 and 0.9 F_1 points on WSJ and Brown test sets respectively. Comparing these values correspondingly to 0.7 and 0.9 point gains by agreement-based co-training with feature split BS shows that the latter has been slightly more promising.

5.5 Co-training by Separate Training Sets

As with confidence-based selection, with this variation of the algorithm, all samples are added to the training set at once. Table 3 shows the performance of the algorithm.

FS	It.	WSJ Test Set						Brown Test Set					
		Constituent-based			Dependency-based			Constituent-based			Dependency-based		
		P	R	F1	P	R	F1	P	R	F1	P	R	F1
UBUS	0	75.6	68.8	72.0	76.3	59.5	66.8	65.1	56.1	60.2	69.0	49.8	57.9
	1	79.0	65.8	**71.8**	77.5	59.8	**67.5**	70.5	53.0	**60.5**	70.6	50.6	**59.0**
UBS	0	75.6	68.8	72.0	73.6	56.9	64.2	65.1	56.1	60.2	66.0	47.7	55.4
	1	78.3	65.4	**71.2**	74.9	58.0	**65.4**	69.4	52.5	**59.8**	69.1	49.8	**57.9**
BS	0	70.4	64.3	67.2	76.3	59.5	66.9	60.7	53.3	56.8	69.0	49.8	57.9
	1	76.1	60.9	**67.6**	78.0	59.3	**67.4**	67.4	50.3	**57.6**	70.5	50.4	**58.8**

Table 2: Co-training Performance with Confidence-based Selection

FS	It.	WSJ Test Set						Brown Test Set					
		Constituent-based			Dependency-based			Constituent-based			Dependency-based		
		P	R	F1	P	R	F1	P	R	F1	P	R	F1
UBUS	0	75.6	68.8	72.0	76.3	59.5	66.9	65.1	56.1	60.2	69.0	49.8	57.9
	1	79.0	59.8	**68.0**	75.5	59.5	**66.6**	70.2	49.3	**57.9**	67.8	50.8	**58.1**
UBS	0	75.6	68.8	72.0	73.6	56.9	64.2	65.1	56.1	60.2	66.0	47.7	55.4
	1	76.7	58.2	**66.2**	73.7	58.1	**65.0**	69.3	49.5	**57.7**	67.2	50.0	**57.3**
BS	0	70.4	64.3	67.2	76.3	59.5	66.9	60.7	53.3	56.8	69.0	49.8	57.9
	1	76.2	57.9	**65.8**	75.1	58.4	**65.7**	67.5	48.8	**56.7**	67.5	49.9	**57.4**

Table 3: Co-training Performance with Separate Training Sets

The constituent-based classifier has been degraded with all feature splits. This even includes balanced and separated feature split (BS), which improved in previous settings.

The dependency-based system, which has always improved before, now degrades when using feature split BS, even on the Brown test set which has been previously benefited with all settings. On the other hand, feature split UBS improves on both test sets, possibly for the same reasons described before. However, the improvement of the dependency-based system with unbalanced feature split is not useful, because the performance of the constituent-based system is much higher, and it does not seem that the dependency-based classifier can reach to (or improve over it) even with more unlabeled data.

It can be seen that this variation of the algorithm performs worse compared to co-training with the common training set. Since in that case, in addition to training on the results of each other, the decision on selecting labeled data is made by both classifiers, this additional cooperation may be the possible reason of this observation.

6 Conclusion and Future Work

This work explores co-training with two views of SRL, namely constituency and dependency. Inspired by the two co-training assumptions, we investigate the performance of the algorithm with three kinds of feature splits: an unbalanced split with some general features in common between feature sets, an unbalanced but fully separated split, and a balanced and fully separated split.

In addition, three variations of the algorithms were examined with all feature splits: agreement-based and confidence-based selection for co-training with common training set, and co-training with separate training sets.

Results showed that the balanced feature split, in which the performances of the classifiers were roughly the same, is more useful for co-training. Moreover, balancing the feature split to reduce performance gap between associated classifiers, is more important than separating feature sets by removing common features.

Also, a common training set proved useful for co-training, unlike separate training sets. However, more experiments are needed to compare agreement- and confidence-based selections.

Due to significant difference between the current work and previous work on SRL co-training described in section 2 comparison is difficult. Nevertheless, unlike He and Gildea (2006), co-training showed to be useful for SRL here, though with slight improvements. In addition, the statistics reported by Lee et al. (2007) are unclear to compare for the reason mentioned in that section. However, as they concluded, more unlabeled data is needed for co-training to be practically useful.

As mentioned, we did not involve parameters like pool, growth size and probability threshold for a step-by-step study. A future work can be to investigate the effect of these parameters. Another direction of future work is to adapt the SRL architecture to better match with the co-training.

References

Abney, S. 2002. Bootstrapping. In *Proceedings of the 40th Annual Meeting of the ACL*, pages 360-367.

Abney, S. 2008. *Semisupervised Learning for Computational Linguistics.* Chapman and Hall, London.

Baker, F., Fillmore, C. and Lowe, J. 1998. The Berkeley FrameNet project. In *Proceedings of COLING-ACL*, pages 86-90.

Blum, A. and Mitchell, T. 1998. Combining Labeled and Unlabeled Data with Co-training. In *Proceedings of the 11th Annual Conference on Computational Learning Theory (COLT '98)*, pages 92-100.

Charniak, E. and Johnson, M. 2005. Coarse-to-fine n-best parsing and MaxEnt discriminative reranking. In *Proceedings of the 43rd Annual Meeting of the ACL*, pages 173-180.

Carreras, X. and Marquez, L. 2004. 'Introduction to the CoNLL-2004 Shared Task: Semantic role labeling', In *Proceedings of the 8th Conference on Computational Natural Language Learning*, pages 89-97.

Carreras, X. and Marquez, L. 2005. Introduction to the CoNLL-2005 shared task: Semantic role labeling. In *Proceedings of the 9th Conference on Natural Language Learning*, pages 152-164.

Clark S., Curran, R. J. and Osborne M. 2003. Bootstrapping POS taggers using Unlabeled Data. In *Proceedings of the 7th Conference on Natural Language Learning at HLT-NAACL*, pages 49-55.

Furstenau, H. and Lapata, M. 2009. Graph Alignment for Semi-Supervised Semantic Role Labeling. In *Proceedings of the 2009 Conference on EMNLP*, pages 11-20.

Gildea, D. and Jurafsky, D. 2002. Automatic labeling of semantic roles. *CL*, 28(3): 245-288.

Gimenez, J. and Marquez, L. 2008. A smorgasbord of features for automatic MT evaluation. In *Proceedings of the 3rd Workshop on Statistical Machine Translation,* ACL, pages 195-198.

Hacioglu, K. 2004. Semantic Role Labeling Using Dependency Trees. In *Proceedings of 20th international Conference on Computational Linguistics.*

He, S. and Gildea, H. 2006. Self-training and Co-training for Semantic Role Labeling: Primary Report. TR 891, University of Colorado at Boulder.

Johansson, R. and Nugues, P. 2008. Dependency-based syntactic-semantic analysis with PropBank and NomBank. In *Proceedings of the 12th Conference on Computational Natural Language Learning*, pages 183-187.

Johansson, R. and Nugues, P. 2007. Extended Constituent-to-dependency Conversion for English. In *Proceedings of NODALIDA 2007*, pages 105-112.

Lee, J., Song, Y. and Rim, H. 2007. Investigation of Weakly Supervised Learning for Semantic Role Labeling. In *Proceedings of the Sixth international Conference on Advanced Language Processing and Web information Technology*, pages 165-170.

Ng, V. and Cardie, C. 2003. Weakly supervised natural language learning without redundant views. In *Proceedings of the 2003 Conference of the HLT-NAACL*, pages 94-101.

Nigam, K. and Ghani, R. 2000. Analyzing the Effectiveness and Applicability of Co-training. In *Proceedings of the 9th conference on Information and knowledge management,* pages 86-93.

Nivre, J. Hall, J. Nilsson, J. Chanev, A. Eryigit, G. Kubler, S. Marinov, S. and Marsi, E. 2007. MaltParser: A Language-independent System for Data-driven Dependency Parsing. *Natural Language Engineering*, 13(2): 95–135.

Palmer, M., Gildea, D. and Kingsbury, P. 2005, The Proposition Bank: A Corpus Annotated with Semantic Roles, *Computational Linguistics*, 31(1).

Pierce, D. and Cardie, C. 2001. Limitations of Co-Training for Natural Language Learning from Large Datasets. In *Proceedings of the 2001 Conference on EMNLP*, pages 1-9.

Koomen, P., Punyakanok, V., Roth, D. and Yi, W. 2005. Generalized inference with multiple semantic role labeling systems. In *Proceedings of the 9th Conference on Natural Language Learning*, pages 181-184.

Sarkar, A. 2001. Applying Co-Training Methods to Statistical Parsing. In *Proceedings of the 2001 Meeting of the North American chapter of the Association for Computational Linguistics*, pages 175-182.

Surdeanu, M., Harabagiu, S., Williams, J. and Aarseth, P. 2003. Using predicate argument structures for information extraction. In *Proceedings of the 41st Annual Meeting of the ACL*, pages 8-15.

Surdeanu, M., Johansson, R., Meyers, A., Marquez, L. and Nivre, J. 2008. The CoNLL 2008 shared task on joint parsing of syntactic and semantic dependencies. In *Proceedings of the 12th Conference on Natural Language Learning*, pages 159-177.

Xue, N. and Palmer, M. 2004. Calibrating Features for Semantic Role Labeling. In *Proceedings of 2004 Conference on Empirical Methods in Natural Language Processing.*

Appendix A. Learning Features

Feature Name	Type	1	2	3	4
Phrase Type	C	√		√	
Path	C	√		√	
Content Word Lemma	C	√		√	
Head Word POS	C	√		√	
Content Word POS	C	√		√	
Governing Category	C	√		√	
Predicate Subcategorization	C	√		√	
Constituent Subcategorization	C	√		√	
Clause+VP+NP Count in Path	C	√		√	
Constituent and Predicate Distance	C	√		√	
Head Word Location in Constituent	C	√		√	
Dependency Relation of Argument Word with Its Head	D		√		√
Dependency Relation of Predicate with Its Head	D		√		√
Lemma of Dependency Head of Argument Word	D		√		√
POS Tag of Dependency Head of Argument Word	D		√		√
Relation Pattern of Predicate's Children	D		√		√
Relation Pattern of Argument Word Children	D		√		√
POS Pattern of Predicate's Children	D		√		√
POS Pattern of Argument Word's Children	D		√		√
Relation Path from Argument Word to Predicate	D		√		√
POS Path from Argument Word to Predicate	D		√		√
Family Relationship between Argument Word and Predicate	D		√		√
POS Tag of Least Common Ancestor of Argument Word and Predicate	D		√		√
POS Path from Argument Word to Least Common Ancestor	D		√		√
Dependency Path Length from Argument Word to Predicate	D		√		√
Whether Argument Word Starts with Capital Letter?	D		√		√
Whether Argument Word is WH word?	D		√		√
Head or Argument Word Lemma	G	√			√
Compound Verb Identifier	G	√			√
Position+Predicate Voice	G	√			√
Predicate Lemma	G	√			√
Predicate POS	G	√		√	

AUTHOR INDEX

Albayrak, Sahin 17
Almedia, J. J. 9
Atalla, Malik 17
Baba, Mohd Sapiyan 41
De Luca, Ernesto William 17
Drury, Brett 9
Kaljahi, Rasoul Samad Zadeh 41
Klinger, Roman 25
Kobayashi, Hayato 33
Leser, Ulf 25
Marecek, David 1
Scheel, Christian 17
Solt, Illes 25
Suzuki, Masaru 33
Thomas, Philippe 25
Torgo, Luis 9
Wakaki, Hiromi 33
Yamasaki, Tomohiro 33
Zabokrtsky, Zdenek 1